CECIL C. KUHNE III

THE LITTLE BOOK *of* HUNTING AND FISHING LAW

AMERICAN BAR ASSOCIATION
Defending Liberty
Pursuing Justice

Cover design by Andrew O. Alcala/ABA Publishing.

15 14 13 12 11 5 4 3 2 1

Library of Congress Cataloging-in-Publication Data

Kuhne, Cecil C., 1952-
The little book of hunting and fishing law / by Cecil C. Kuhne III.
p. cm.
Includes bibliographical references and index.
ISBN 978-1-61632-891-7 (alk. paper)
1. Game laws--United States--Cases. 2. Fishery law and legislation--United States--Cases.
3. Wildlife conservation--Law and legislation--United States. I. Title.
KF5640.K848 2011
346.7304'69549--dc22

2011016134

Discounts are available for books ordered in bulk. Special consideration is given to state bars, CLE programs, and other bar-related organizations. Inquire at Book Publishing, ABA Publishing, American Bar Association, 321 North Clark Street, Chicago, Illinois 60654-7598.

www.ababooks.org

Table of Contents

Introduction

Hunting and fishing endeavors seem so deliciously straightforward. Slowly pull the trigger. Quickly release the line.

The simplicity of these popular outdoor pursuits is a pleasant contrast to the complexity of modern-day life. These pastimes are practiced every day by millions of zealous advocates around the globe, and at times, the fervor in which they are engaged verges on the religious.

But with so many people participating in this hook-and-bullet arena, things are bound to go horribly wrong. And that is exactly the point, of course, where the law—and (fortunately) lawyers—come in.

There are, naturally, the *personal injuries* that can result in these feverish activities. Unfortunately, hunters (and sometimes even passersby) are sometimes shot by other hunters, and fishermen occasionally hook other fishermen. These lamentable accidents often lead to interesting cases of litigation that attempt to answer such knotty questions as:

- Can a poacher shot by the landowner for his transgression then recover from the landowner for his injuries?
- Can a fisherman who is accidentally injured by an errant hook of another fisherman recover for his damages?
- Can a jogger who is randomly shot by a hunter on public land sue the city for negligence in preventing such accidents?
- Can a hunter in a hunting party be held liable for negligence in supervising his fellow hunter?

Violations of fish and game laws—and the resulting *criminal offenses*—occasionally occur, and several thorny issues arise, such as:

- Can a game warden set up a roadblock to "snag" fishermen who possess more than their legal limit?

- Can a fisherman defeat a conviction for using an illegal fishing device if he is caught red-handed by the game warden?
- Can a hunter, who can legally trespass onto unposted agricultural land in order to recover a deer he shot, do so if he is specifically told by the landowner not to?

There are also the potential problems of *product liability* and *commercial loss*, as shown by cases that attempt to determine such intriguing questions as:

- Can a shotgun manufacturer be held liable for punitive damages in the event of an exploding barrel?
- Can the owner of a commercial fishing operation recover for lost profits that occur as the result of a boating accident that is the fault of another boater?

The whole realm of *intellectual property* with regard to hunting and fishing equipment frequently presents some vexatious dilemmas:

- Can the ubiquitous term "Safari" be exclusively reserved by a manufacturer for a line of hunting clothes and boots?
- Can fishing rods be exclusively trademarked simply because they are the color green?

And then there are the intriguing questions of *freedom of religion* that sometimes arise in the world of fish and game:

- Can a law requiring hunters to wear safety orange infringe the Constitution's free exercise clause when one's religion discourages the wearing of such vivid clothing?
- Can religious animal sacrifice be held to a different standard than hunting?

The cases assembled in the book you hold in your hand struggle with these and myriad other issues of interest to those who are fortunate enough to wield guns and rods. In the process, these decisions amply prove two very important propositions: (1) the legal maze is far more intimidating and dangerous than the natural world, and (2) the greatest *outdoor* drama often occurs *inside* the courtroom.

The Little Book *of* Hunting and Fishing Law

Chapter One

Poaching:
The Shootout at the O.K. Corral

Kelly v. Smith, 485 F.2d 520 (5th Cir. 1973)

The broad, mud-filled waters of the lower Mississippi River are amply dotted with hundreds of thick, vegetated islands. Many of them are notoriously full of wild game, making them prime targets for the trigger-happy aspirations of hunters.

For those so inclined, a clear autumnal day among these environs is ideal for stalking deer, and in the Deep South such ritual outings often approach the level of a cultural, nay, almost spiritual, pastime.

A hunter by the name of Allen Kelly, along with his three sons, desperately wanted to take advantage of these near-ideal hunting conditions, and the four men had their eyes set on a remote, and privately owned, strip of land called Woodstock Island. Situated in the middle of the Mississippi River between the states of Mississippi and Arkansas, Woodstock had an enviable reputation for hunting greatness. Unfortunately, the Kellys did not have permission to hunt the island, as those privileges were reserved for members of an exclusive private hunting club.

Clad in camouflage and possessed of all the necessary weapons for a foray in the woods, the four Kellys (all of whom were residents of the state of Mississippi) quietly slipped across the sweeping river toward the dense banks of the island in their motorized, 15-foot galvanized-aluminum boat. In store lay a day of trespassing at the very least, and if they were as lucky as they hoped, some successful poaching for the massive deer that reportedly inhabited these reaches. Little did the Kellys know that they *themselves* would soon become the objects of gunfire.

Woodstock was owned by Anderson-Tully Lumber Company, which had granted to an Arkansas land management concern called Chicot Land Company a license for exclusive hunting rights. In return, Chicot paid a fee, maintained the roads, and assumed general responsibility for the well-being of the island. J. C. Smith, a resident of Arkansas, had been the island's caretaker for the past thirty years. He was also the prime mover in organizing and running the hunting club.

On the day in question, J. C. Smith and a hunting club member named Bledsoe were relaxing at the rustic clubhouse, enjoying the beautiful fall weather and perhaps an adult beverage or two. Another club member, who just happened to be approaching the island in his small airplane, sighted the Kellys' boat tied to shore. In an era before cell phones, he wanted to contact Smith and Bledsoe about this unfortunate development, so he dropped from his plane a plastic tube containing a note that informed his colleagues of the suspected trespassers.

Smith and Bledsoe immediately headed toward the poachers. The Kellys, now acutely aware that they had been caught *in flagrante*, scurried toward their small boat in an attempt to flee the island.

As Smith and Bledsoe arrived at the dock, the Kellys' craft was already in the water, speeding away as quickly as it could under its heavy load. It is undisputed that gunfire eventually ensued, but who actually *initiated* the altercation is a point where the parties' stories diverge.

Smith and Bledsoe claimed that they politely asked the Kellys to return to the island in order to establish their identity, and that the Kellys responded in an unfriendly way by shooting at them. The Kellys, however, contended it was Smith and Bledsoe who fired the first shots. The lower court believed the Kellys.

In any event, a solid rifle shot from shore was eventually fired *across* the bow of the Kellys' boat to signal it to stop. It continued on. The gunners lowered their sights and then fired into the water *beside* the boat. It throttled away at full speed. The next rounds were apparently fired *into* the boat, where they solidly struck two of the men inside. The poachers, having suffered serious casualties, then dispatched a few rounds toward the bank in a show of self-defense.

Almost six years later (the court explained that they "had difficulty finding competent counsel"), Allen Kelly and his son, Garland, filed suit for their injuries in federal district court against Anderson-Tully, Chicot, Smith, and Bledsoe, alleging diversity of citizenship and admiralty jurisdiction. (Mississippi had a one-year statute of limitaions for assault and battery, so the case would have been barred in state court.)

The central issue was whether the tort claims of the Kellys for their injuries were within federal admiralty jurisdiction. After a nonjury trial, the district court concluded that despite the Kellys' status as trespassers, Chicot, Smith, and Bledsoe were jointly and severally liable to Allen Kelly for $69,772.40 and to Garland Kelly for $2,593.96.

The issue of jurisdiction was critical to the Kellys' claim. Historically, the standard for determination of maritime tort jurisdiction was viewed as a question of locality. Maritime law governs only those actions where the "substance and consummation of the injury" takes place on navigable waters. The strict locality standard had been repeated with such frequency that most courts

were unaware of the fact that the Supreme Court had never explicitly decided whether maritime tort jurisdiction turned solely on locality.

The Supreme Court eventually dealt with the issue in a case where the plaintiff's airplane lost power from ingesting seagulls into its engines while taking off from the defendant's airport. The plane came to rest and then sank at the end of the runway in Lake Erie. The plaintiff sued in admiralty, alleging that the defendant negligently failed to keep its runway free of gulls or to warn of their presence. The court of appeals found the tort occurred on land and was therefore *not* cognizable in admiralty. The Supreme Court therefore faced the broader question of whether maritime locality alone is sufficient to create admiralty tort jurisdiction.

In that particular case, the Supreme Court declared that the mere fact the alleged wrong "occurred" over navigable waters was not itself sufficient to turn an airplane negligence case into a maritime tort. It was, the Court suggested, far more consistent with the history and purpose of admiralty to require that the malfeasance bear a more significant relationship to traditional maritime activity than a purely mechanical application of the rule allowed. The Court recognized that superficial similarities might exist between the plights of sinking ships and airplanes downed on water, but it pointed out that the plane's unexpected descent in that case was *not* attributable to a cause related to the sea.

The Fifth Circuit had itself also previously recognized the inadequacies of the strict locality test. It too concluded that the facts of the claim must bear a *substantial* connection to maritime activities in order to invoke federal admiralty jurisdiction. In a whiplash-neck and back-injury case involving a rear-end car collision on a floating pontoon-ferry, the court focused on the relationship of the maritime activities to the parties, to the nature and apparent cause of the accident, and to the injury sustained. Finding that a rear-end collision between terrestrial vehicles, operated by landlubbers, and resulting in a typical automobile accident lacked a sufficient maritime connection, they concluded that admiralty jurisdiction was *not* appropriate.

In the present case, the Fifth Circuit found that the stretch of the Mississippi River where the Kellys were injured was in fact navigable (evidence of navigability included testimony by a tugboat captain who regularly traveled it). However, the court determined that admiralty jurisdiction did not arise from the mere fact that the Kellys' injury occurred on navigable waters while they were inside a boat. Those facts may have been persuasive in granting maritime jurisdiction, but the court looked at *all* the circumstances for a substantial maritime relationship: the functions and roles of the parties, the types of vehicles and instrumentalities involved, the causation and the type of injury, and traditional concepts of the role of admiralty law.

The court noted that the party most seriously injured in the gunfire exchange was the pilot of the boat—the person responsible for safe navigation of the river. The vehicle involved was also a boat (not an automobile or an airplane), and its function was transportation across navigable waters—a traditional role of watercraft. The other instrumentalities involved—firearms—and the injuries they caused, were deemed not so inherently indigenous to land as to preclude a maritime connection. Additionally, upholding admiralty jurisdiction did not distort long-evolved principles of maritime law. Admiralty has traditionally been concerned with furnishing remedies for those injured while traveling navigable waters.

The court also concluded that public policy militated toward granting admiralty jurisdiction. The admiralty jurisdiction of federal courts stems from the important national interest in uniformity of law and remedies for those facing the hazards of waterborne transportation. Rifle fire directed at a vessel, even a small one, on a major commercial artery, and injuring the pilot, presented sufficient danger to maritime commerce for the federal courts of admiralty to assume jurisdiction and furnish remedies to those aboard the vessel and injured by that conduct. The court remarked that regardless of whether the Kellys had available remedies in state courts, the federal interest in protecting navigation on the Mississippi River overrode any considerations of federal-state comity or conflicts of interest.

And so, oddly enough, the shoot-out at the O.K. Corral suddenly became . . . a maritime tort.

Hook & Bullet

Teddy Roosevelt's Beloved Rifle

The ranchman owes to his rifle not only the keen pleasure and strong excitement of the chase, but also much of his bodily comfort; for, save for his prowess as a hunter and his skill as a marksman with this, his favorite weapon, he would almost always be sadly stinted for fresh meat. Now that the buffalo have gone, and the Sharps rifle by which they were destroyed is also gone, almost all ranchmen use some form of repeater. Personally, I prefer the Winchester, using the new model, with a 45-caliber bullet of 300 grains, backed by 90 grains of powder, or else falling back on my faithful old stand-by, the 45-75. But the truth is that all good modern rifles are efficient weapons; it is the man behind the gun that makes the difference. An inch or two in trajectory or a second or two in rapidity of fire is as nothing compared to sureness of eye and steadiness of hand.

From April to August antelope are the game we chiefly follow, killing only the bucks; after that season, black-tail and white-tail

Hook & Bullet (continued)

deer. Now and then we get a chance at mountain sheep, and more rarely at larger game still. As a rule, I never shoot anything but bucks. But in the rutting season, when the bucks' flesh is poor, or when we need to lay in a good stock of meat for the winter, this rule of course must be broken.

The smoked venison stored away in the fall lasts us through the bitter weather, as well as through the even less attractive period covering the first weeks of spring. At that time we go out as little as possible. The roads are mere morasses, crusted after nightfall with a shell of thin ice, through which the shaggy horses break heavily. Walking is exceedingly tiresome, the boots becoming caked with masses of adhesive clay. The deer stay with us all the time; but they are now in poor condition, the does heavy with fawn and the bucks with ungrown antlers.

Antelope gather together in great bands in the fall, and either travel south, leaving the country altogether, or else go to some out-of-the-way place where they are not likely to be disturbed. Antelope are queer, freaky beasts, and it is hard to explain why, when most of these great bands go off south, one or two always stay in the Bad Lands. Such a band having chosen its wintering ground, which is usually in a valley or on a range of wide plateaus, will leave it only with great reluctance, and if it is discovered by hunters most of its members will surely be butchered before the survivors are willing to abandon the place and seek new quarters.

From *Ranch Life and the Hunting Trail*, by Theodore Roosevelt (1896)

Chapter Two

Accidental Shooting:

The Case for Vicarious Liability

Montgomery v. Remsburg, 810 A.2d 14 (Md. 2002)

On a crisp opening day of deer season, Charles Montgomery and his son Brian hid patiently in the underbrush of the family's farm in western Maryland. While they waited in the quiet darkness before sunrise, they were surprised to hear the voices of other hunters approaching them from the north.

The Montgomerys remained out of sight of the encroaching hunters. The trespassers, it transpired, were well-known to the Montgomerys. They included James Remsburg Sr. and his 27-year-old son, James Remsburg Jr., along with three friends. Remsburg Junior climbed into a tree stand that had been located for many years on the Montgomery property.

A few minutes later the Montgomerys decided to quietly leave their hiding place due to the now overcrowded scene. As they left, Charles Montgomery reached down to massage a leg cramp.

Remsburg Junior, who in the still-dark conditions apparently mistook Charles Montgomery for a deer, fired a single shell from his shotgun. The shot grazed Brian Montgomery's neck and then soundly pierced Charles Montgomery's right arm and side.

As soon as he realized his mistake, Remsburg Junior called out to his father, who left his post in a tree stand on the neighboring property. The five trespassers arrived to find Charles Montgomery bleeding profusely. Seeing the injured hunters, Remsburg Senior awkwardly exclaimed, "I guess that rules out telling Jamie to shoot at the first thing that moves."

As a result of the gunshot injury, Charles Montgomery lost almost all use of his right arm and shoulder, and retained only limited use of his right hand. The Montgomerys sued both of the Remsburgs for negligence. After they settled with Remsburg Junior, they continued to pursue their claims against Remsburg Senior.

The circuit court granted summary judgment in favor of Remsburg Senior, finding that he could not be held liable for negligence because he had no duty to (a) warn the Montgomerys that they would be hunting in the area or (b) prevent his son from shooting the Montgomerys on their own property.

This appeal presented an issue of first impression in Maryland, as it concerned the liability of a hunter for his hunting companion's mistaken shooting of another. As a general rule, hunters are *not* liable for negligent and illegal acts of their hunting companions.

In the circumstances presented here, however, the appellate court held that there were factual disputes related to determining whether Remsburg Senior owed the Montgomerys a *special* duty to take preventive measures—either by informing the Montgomerys that they intended to hunt in that area, or by giving Remsburg Junior enough information to alert him to the possibility that other hunters might be present. Because the trial court premised its grant of summary judgment solely on its "no duty" holding, the appellate court reversed the judgment and remanded for further proceedings.

The appellate court's review of the summary judgment record necessarily reflected the facts and inferences most favorable to the Montgomerys. When Remsburg Junior fired at the Montgomerys, he was located on their property. In contrast, Remsburg Senior was not. Instead, he was positioned in a tree stand located on the adjacent property and some 300 or 400 yards from his son. The other members of the Remsburgs' hunting party were also located on the adjacent property.

The Montgomerys and Remsburgs were not strangers. Remsburg Senior had a long relationship with Charles Montgomery's late father, James, as well as years of hunting experience on the Montgomery property. James Montgomery and Remsburg Senior had previously entered into a five-year written hunting lease.

When the Remsburgs' lease expired, Charles Montgomery assumed his father's role as the decision maker regarding hunting rights. Charles verbally granted Remsburg Senior hunting rights in each of the ensuing years. During these years, Remsburg Senior often brought his son and others to hunt on the Montgomery property. In fact, while Remsburg Junior was still a minor, he and his father built the tree stand from which he eventually shot at the Montgomerys. This stand was located, at the suggestion of James Montgomery, near the northern boundary of their property.

As the current deer-hunting season approached, Charles Montgomery decided not to give Remsburg Senior permission to hunt on his property. He claimed that he made the decision, in part, because there had been reports of hunting altercations involving Remsburg Senior.

However, Remsburg Senior never spoke with Charles Montgomery about hunting rights for the current season, but instead entered into a written lease for hunting rights on the adjacent property to the north. Whether Remsburg Senior also had a right

to hunt on the Montgomery property was disputed. Remsburg Junior asserted a right to hunt from the tree stand on the Montgomery property that was derived from his father's hunting rights under a written lease, which he alleged had been renewed for another five years.

The Montgomerys denied that the written lease was renewed, and they asserted that Remsburg Senior never paid any rent for such a renewal. In addition, they contended that, even if the lease had been renewed, it never covered the portion of their property where the tree stand was located.

The Montgomerys also pointed to other evidence showing that Remsburg Senior appreciated the potential for trouble if his hunting party hunted from the Montgomery's tree stand. They presented testimony of a hunter who reported that he had confronted Remsburg Senior about illegally hunting on the Montgomery's property.

The Montgomerys also contended that on the night before deer season opened, Remsburg Senior telephoned Charles Montgomery's house to ask for permission to hunt, but no one was home. Remsburg Senior also apparently never mentioned to his hunting party that he had failed to speak with the Montgomerys about hunting rights for the current season.

The circuit court held that summary judgment was appropriate on the Montgomerys' negligence claim, because Remsburg Senior's duty would have to arise out of a special relationship, of which they concluded there was none. The Montgomerys' negligence claim against Remsburg Senior rested on the contention that Remsburg Senior had a special duty to take measures that would have prevented the accidental shooting. In effect, they argued that Remsburg Senior was negligent in failing either to control his son or to warn them of his presence.

The Montgomerys asserted that all three of the potential sources of special duty were present. They claimed that Remsburg Senior had a special duty based on (1) Maryland's hunting laws, (2) the long course of contractual dealing between Remsburg Senior and the Montgomerys, and (3) Remsburg Senior's leadership of the hunting party. They argued that Remsburg Senior had a sufficient relationship to the Montgomerys and control over the hunting conducted by his son to create a duty to the Montgomerys to warn and to take reasonable actions to assure their safety.

The Montgomerys argued that the circuit court erred in determining that the existence of a special relationship creating a tort duty was an issue of law, because that issue is a matter of *factual* determination to be decided by the trier of fact. They asserted that if there was any set of facts on which the special relationship could be found by a reasonable jury, the issue should have been resolved at trial.

The appellate court held that *as a matter of law* the organizer and leader of a hunting party does not assume, by virtue of that role, a duty to instruct all the hunters in the party about basic hunting safety rules, including the point at which shooting may legally begin. Second, they agreed that the head of a hunting party generally does not have a duty to supervise members of the party during the hunt. Third, they held that a member of the hunting party who does nothing to actively encourage another to take an illegal or negligent shot has no duty to the person hit by that shot. Fourth, they agreed that a member of a hunting party who does not induce another hunter to reasonably believe that no other hunters will be in the vicinity has no duty to the shooting victim.

Nevertheless, they concluded in this case that there were disputed facts and inferences that, when resolved in favor of the Montgomerys, should have prevented the court from entering summary judgment in favor of Remsburg Senior.

The appellate court agreed that it could *not* usurp the role of the jury in determining whether a special duty exists. If there are disputed facts or inferences about whether a special relationship exists, those disputes have to be resolved before the court can decide whether there is a special duty. It is for the *court* to determine, as a matter of law, what characteristics must be present for a relationship to give rise to a duty, the breach of which may result in tort liability. It is then for the *jury* to determine whether the facts establish the elements of that relationship.

The court cited a Wisconsin case in support of its decision. In that case, the leader of a deer hunting party invited a 15-year-old minor who had completed hunter education and firearm safety courses, had hunted "numerous times" (including by himself), and was licensed and legally "permitted to hunt without adult supervision." The leader of the hunting party told the minor where to sit and other general suggestions. He did not, however, tell the minor about a nearby path that was used by other hunters seeking access to nearby hunting areas, nor did he tell the minor to wait for the official start of hunting season or for sufficient light before firing his gun.

While it was still dark and before the official start of the hunting season, the minor observed what he believed to be a group of deer walking up the trail. It was in fact a group of hunters. The minor fired his weapon and killed one of the hunters. The widow of the deceased hunter sued the minor, his insurer, and the leader of the hunting party. The trial court granted summary judgment in favor of the leader of the hunting party on the ground that he owed no duty to the deceased, and that there was no evidence of causal negligence.

On appeal, the widow argued (1) that the leader of the hunting party had a duty to instruct the minor about hunting rules against shooting too early and without adequate visibility, and (2) that he had a duty to supervise the minor, a member of his hunting party. The widow also suggested that the leader of the hunting party actively misled the minor into shooting before the official start of the season and induced the erroneous belief that no one else would be in the area.

Rejecting all these arguments, the Wisconsin appellate court affirmed the judgment because there was no duty owed by the leader of the hunting party. The court first considered whether an adult hunter, who was not the child's parent, had a duty to supervise or instruct a fifteen-year-old certified and experienced hunter who was a member of the adult's hunting party. It answered that question in the negative because it was not reasonably foreseeable that the minor would flagrantly violate hunting rules he knew and understood. The court specifically rejected the contention that the leader of the hunting party must ensure that an independent member of his party comply with fundamental hunting safety rules by giving pre-hunt instructions.

The present court found the Wisconsin decision persuasive, though it eventually reached a different result. It applied the Wisconsin court's general principles limiting the liability of hunters for the negligent and illegal acts of their hunting companions, but ultimately concluded that the decision as to whether a hunter has stepped outside the safe harbor of those limitations could *not* be resolved as a matter of law.

The court held that there was enough evidence to raise an inference that Remsburg Senior breached a duty of care to the Montgomerys by inducing Remsburg Junior to believe that no other hunters would be in the vicinity. A jury could reasonably conclude that Remsburg Junior was hunting from the tree stand under the mistaken belief that the Montgomerys would *not* be hunting in that area because they had granted Remsburg Senior permission to hunt there.

A jury could also conclude that Remsburg Senior was aware that his son did not expect anyone else to be near the tree stand, even though Remsburg Senior knew from a recent encounter with another hunter that the Montgomerys might in fact be hunting there that morning. By giving his son "permission" to use the tree stand, without (a) telling him that it was on the Montgomery's property, (b) warning him that the Montgomerys had not given him the right to hunt on their property, (c) warning him that the Montgomerys were not aware of their plans to hunt on their property, and (d) warning him that the Montgomerys had granted hunting rights to others, Remsburg Senior may have negligently induced his son to believe that no other hunters would be in the vicinity.

For these reasons, the court held that the principles generally limiting a hunter's liability for the negligence of a hunting companion did not warrant summary judgment in favor of Remsburg Senior. The court reasoned that its decision preserved the resolution of factual disputes for the jury, while ensuring that hunters may be held liable for damages inflicted by their hunting companions *only* when their own acts or omissions bring about that companion's injurious conduct.

The moral of the story? Should you ever decide to take your son hunting, be sure to (1) tell him that you are in fact trespassing on another person's land, and (2) let him know that it might be a good idea *not* to shoot the property owner.

Hook & Bullet

Lion Hunt

The ground was fairly open round our tree, with only a small bush every here and there; and from our position it was a most fascinating sight to watch this great brute stealing stealthily round us, taking advantage of every bit of cover as he came. His skill showed that he was an old hand at the terrible game of man-hunting: so I determined to run no undue risk of losing him this time. I accordingly waited until he got quite close—about twenty yards away—and then fired my .303 at his chest. I heard the bullet strike him, but unfortunately it had no knockdown effect, for with a fierce growl he turned and made off with great long bounds. Before he disappeared from sight, however, I managed to have three more shots at him from the magazine rifle, and another growl told me that the last of these had also taken effect.

We awaited daylight with impatience, and at the first glimmer of dawn we set out to hunt him down. I took a native tracker with me, so that I was free to keep a good look-out, while Mahina followed immediately behind with a Martini carbine. Splashes of blood being plentiful, we were able to get along quickly; and we had not proceeded more than a quarter of a mile through the jungle when suddenly a fierce warning growl was heard right in front of us. Looking cautiously through the bushes, I could see the man-eater glaring out in our direction, and showing his tusks in an angry snarl. I at once took careful aim and fired. Instantly he sprang out and made a most determined charge down on us.

I fired again and knocked him over; but in a second he was up once more and coming for me as fast as he could in his crippled condition. A third shot had no apparent effect, so I put out my hand for the Martini, hoping to stop him with it. To my dismay, it was not there. The terror of the sudden charge had proved too much for Mahina, and both he and the carbine were by this time well on their way up a tree. In the circumstances there was nothing to do but follow suit, which I did without loss of time: and but for the fact that one of my shots had broken a hind leg, the brute would most certainly have had me. Even as it was, I had barely time to swing myself up out of his reach before he arrived at the foot of the tree.

When the lion found he was too late, he started to limp back to the thicket; but by this time I had seized the carbine from Mahina, and the first shot I fired from it seemed to give him his quietus, for he fell over and lay motionless. Rather foolishly, I at once scrambled down from the tree and walked up towards him. To my surprise and no little alarm he jumped up and attempted another charge. This time, however, a Martini bullet in the chest and another in the head finished him for good and all; he dropped in his tracks not five yards away from me, and died gamely, biting savagely at a branch which had fallen to the ground.

From *The Man-Eaters of Tsavo*, by John Henry Patterson (1907)

Chapter Three

Beware the Game Warden:

Search and Seizure Issues

State v. Sherburne, 571 A.2d 1181 (Me. 1990)

One fine spring day in May, officers of the Maine Warden Service established a roadblock to enforce the state's fishing laws.

Donald and Gary Sherburne were returning from a successful three-day fishing trip at Lake Chesuncook when they were stopped. They were travelling in a truck owned and operated by Donald, and they were towing a motorboat owned by Gary. Since routine inspections were made of any vehicle towing a boat, the Sherburnes were directed to the designated inspection area.

After entering the checkpoint, the game warden approached Donald and requested permission to check his fish and his gear. Donald enthusiastically agreed, reassuring the officer nonchalantly that they had their "legal limit." Gary promptly produced for the warden's inspection a cooler containing four foil-wrapped fish (coincidentally, the daily limit for two people).

The warden proceeded to board the boat. Despite urgent assurances from Donald that the cooler contained their total catch, the warden searched three closed compartments located in the bow of Gary's boat. In the third compartment, he unfortunately found a plastic bag that contained fifteen salmon.

Gary readily admitted to placing the bag in the compartment, but with some adroitness explained that the fish just happened to belong to other members of their fishing party who, conveniently enough, were not present. In spite of this skillful explanation, the warden cited each of the Sherburnes for possession of fifteen fish in excess of regulations of the Department of Inland Fisheries and Wildlife, requiring them to pay a hefty fine. The Sherburnes' fish dinner that night must have tasted a little . . . expensive.

The Sherburnes appealed the decision of the superior court affirming their convictions in the district court. The Sherburnes contended in the appellate court that the evidence used against them, secured as the result of the roadblock, should have been suppressed. They further maintained that there was insufficient evidence of their possession of illegal fish and that the fine imposed was egregious.

The Sherburnes maintained, above all, that their constitutional right to be free of unreasonable searches and seizures had been violated by the roadblock and the ensuing search. The district court denied these motions, determining that the roadblock was conducted "consistently and reasonably" and that the Sherburnes consented to the search. The roadblock in this case, designed to promote compliance with Maine's fish and wildlife laws and regulations, no doubt constituted a seizure under the Fourth Amendment to the United States Constitution. It had to be tested, as are all roadblocks intended to discover and deter motor-vehicle violations, by "balancing the intrusion on the individual's Fourth Amendment interests against the promotion of legitimate governmental interests."

In deciding whether a brief stop at a regulatory roadblock violates a citizen's Fourth Amendment rights, the courts consider the reasonableness of the action under the factors set forth below:

- the degree of discretion, if any, left to the officer in the field;
- the location of the roadblock;
- the time and duration of the roadblock;
- the standards set by superior officers;
- the advance notice to the public;
- advance warning to the individual approaching motorist;
- the maintenance of safety conditions;
- the degree of fear or anxiety generated by the operation;
- the average length of time each motorist is detained;
- the physical factors surrounding the location, type, and method of operation;
- the availability of less intrusive methods;
- the degree of effectiveness of the procedure; and
- any other relevant circumstances.

The location for the roadblock in this case was chosen by an eighteen-year veteran of the department based upon his experience that the route was one heavily travelled by fishermen. The particular spot was the site of an earlier roadblock that disclosed numerous violations governing size, weight, and number of fish. Additionally, the area for the roadblock provided adequate space to direct vehicles off the road, and the timing of the operation (scheduled for a Sunday afternoon during peak fishing season) was approved by a superior officer.

In conformity with a written policy of the department, a sign was posted advising motorists that they would be stopped and inspected. A police vehicle was parked beside the southbound travel lane, the site of the checkpoint that was marked by orange safety cones. An officer stationed there made a routine inquiry of all vehicles passing through the checkpoint. That officer determined, in light of responses given by the vehicles' occupants and

the presence of "obvious signs of fishing activity," whether further inquiry and inspection were warranted. In those instances, vehicles were directed to pull off the highway into an inspection area. There one of the wardens conducted further inspections. Sixty violations were cited at the checkpoint that day.

Utilizing a rigorous approach, the courts have upheld roadblock stops that furthered important governmental objectives when conducted in conformity with procedures that minimized intrusions on protected interests. In weighing the governmental interests advanced by a roadblock of this type, the courts have examined the societal interest in dealing with the issue effectively, the availability of less intrusive means to accomplish the objective, and the efficacy of the method chosen.

The courts have long recognized that the laws designed to protect and preserve fish and game reflect their importance and value to the state. Roadblocks have been upheld as a means of enforcing game and wildlife laws designed to promote conservation. In determining whether a less intrusive method would adequately serve the important conservation purpose furthered by a roadblock of this type, the courts recognize the difficult task with which fish and game enforcement officers are charged. That task includes the responsibility for enforcement of fish and game laws with limited numbers of personnel over a wide territory, much of which is uninhabited, and justifies the method chosen.

In the present case, the Sherburnes argued that the roadblock was not conducted reasonably because the wardens failed to comply with the department's policy directive on checkpoints and inspections requiring that *all* vehicles be stopped and inspected. They maintained that the determination that a further inquiry and inspection was necessary amounted to a discretionary examination of the type condemned in previous decisions. The court disagreed.

Though the department policy provided that all vehicles should be stopped and inspected, it implicitly countenanced that more extensive inquiries might be undertaken through its provision of inspection techniques for both threshold inquiries and further inspections. The courts have approved the use of further inspections where the circumstances warranted the adoption of that approach. In the present case, the court held that the roadblock was conducted reasonably.

The Sherburnes next contended that the trial court erred in finding that consent was given to the warrantless search of the boat. They argued that any consent given by Donald was ineffective to authorize the search of the boat owned by Gary. They further contended that any consent was given under "inherently coercive" circumstances and thus was presumptively invalid.

In order for consent to be considered valid, the courts have required that it be given voluntarily by one "with an appropriate relationship" to the property to be searched. Irrespective of whether Donald had either sufficient authority to make his consent to search the boat binding on Gary, the court held that the actions of Gary alone were sufficient to allow the court to infer consent. Gary, the boat's owner, cooperated with the game warden's request to check "fish and gear" by boarding the boat with him and producing the cooler.

The Sherburnes' argument that any consent was involuntary was based on the fact that a number of uniformed wardens or police were present in the inspection area, and that the Sherburnes were not informed that they could refuse the warden's request. Although there were a number of officers in the area, their activity was not focused on the Sherburnes. The Sherburne vehicle was only one of 3,200 vehicles stopped that day, and only one game warden approached and engaged the Sherburnes while in the inspection area. The warden testified that he intended to search only if allowed.

Furthermore, the courts have not required that knowledge of a right to object to an officer's search request is necessary in order to establish the validity of consent. Competent evidence existed to support the trial court's finding that the search was in fact conducted with the consent of the Sherburnes.

The convictions were thus affirmed. One can only wonder whether, the next time the Sherburnes possessed a cooler full of contraband fish, they took a different route home.

Hook & Bullet

Rising Trout

I was warned that at this season of the year, when the water was low, I must not expect to catch any of these fish, but I cared nothing for warnings. The trout were there, and were rising, and though I saw at once that it was a case for dry fly and for that only, I had by this time been taught to believe that any one, who could catch Winchester trout, could catch rising trout anywhere. These trout, however, at first upset my calculations. They brought me face to face with a difficulty which did not exist on the ticket water at Winchester—they were unapproachable. Never was an angler more put upon his mettle. There were trout visibly and audibly rising, which had never seen an artificial dry fly, and would probably take it at once. They were evidently also big trout. There was splendid sport to be had, and reputation and glory to be won in catching even one of them, and yet so shy were they, that I could not get my dry fly to them.

For two days they defeated me utterly. I walked and knelt and waded and labored and perspired under an August sun without success. Some of the trout were put down by my

Hook & Bullet (continued)

approach, some were scared by the first waving of the rod, and some, which had been successfully stalked, turned tail and fled when the gut floated over them without even the last drag; at last, on the second evening in a fading light, I hooked a fish which went off upstream at once with a mighty rush, and came to rest somewhere out of sight at the end of a lot of line. I waded carefully up in the twilight, keeping a tight line by reeling up as I went till I was over a great bed of strong weeds.

Into this one hand carefully felt its way along the casting line, and touched at last the side of a great fish. Nothing could be seen for it was getting dark, and the weeds were too thick for a landing net to be used in them. I tried with one hand to arrange a grip on the trout, and very broad and hard he felt; but at the critical moment he made the most violent commotion in the weeds and dashed of somewhere. When all was still I felt again and found in the weeds only the end of broken gut. There was nothing more to be done that evening, and I waded out and lay on the bank in the dusk. On the whole, I think that was the bitterest moment I have ever known in angling. To have come so near to success, and to have it snatched from me at the last moment, after keenness and effort had been sustained at the very highest pitch for two whole days, was more than could be borne.

But success did come afterwards, and in broad daylight; I found a place where, by wading and kneeling in the river on the shallow side, it was possible to get within reach of and opposite to rising trout without frightening them. Then the fly could be thrown some way above them with an underhand cast, so as not to show the rod; and being opposite and not below, I could let the fly float down a few inches on the near side of a rising trout, so that only the fly and none of the gut was seen. In this way I at last caught one or two trout, and then somehow, when the frost of failure had once broken up, it seemed more easy to succeed all over the river.

From *Fly Fishing*, by Edward Grey (1901)

Chapter Four

Exploding Shotguns:
Punitive Damage Issues

Loitz v. Remington Arms Co.,
563 N.E.2d 397 (Ill. 1990)

Robert Loitz was competing in a summer trapshooting event at his local gun club in central Illinois when the accident occurred.

An experienced marksman, Loitz was using a 12-gauge shotgun made by Remington and sold as the Model 1100. This is a semiautomatic, gas-operated firearm, and it was designed for both target shooting and for hunting game. At the time of the incident, more than three million versions of the Model 1100 had been manufactured. Loitz bought his gun secondhand, and he had fired more than sixty rounds through it without a glitch. But the next shot was a little different—the barrel exploded.

The shells being used by Loitz on the day of the accident were ones he had reloaded himself. Reloaded shells are commonly used by competitive shooters, and they are naturally less expensive than factory-made ammunition. Whether these homemade shells were the cause of the explosion was an important issue at trial.

Following the accident, Loitz underwent reconstructive surgery on his left hand. He incurred damages of about $5,000 in medical expenses, and he lost significant time from work. Loitz brought suit against Remington for both negligence and for willful and wanton misconduct, and he requested awards of compensatory and punitive damages.

The central issue at trial was the safety and suitability of the metal used in the barrel of the Model 1100. The barrel is made from a type of steel known as American Iron and Steel Institute (AISI) 1140 modified. This steel contains manganese sulfide and is described as free-machining steel, which means that it can be worked more easily. In the manufacturing process used by Remington, each shotgun barrel begins as a slug of steel and is forged and worked until a barrel is produced. After the gun is fully assembled, it is subjected to extensive testing.

In Remington's testing procedure, a single round capable of producing higher-than-normal pressure is fired from the gun. Afterward, the gun is inspected visually for signs of damage, and several normal rounds are later discharged. From the evidence presented at trial, it appeared that normal shotgun shells would produce pressures in a range between 8,000 and 12,000 pounds per square inch. The proof-test shells used by Remington produced pressures ranging from 18,000 to 22,000 pounds. Remington contended that Loitz's gun exploded because it was subjected to a pressure of approximately 60,000 pounds.

Loitz's expert witness, a professor of metallurgy at the University of Illinois, testified that the gun barrel exploded because of fatigue failure in response to a normal-pressure shell. In his opinion, AISI 1140 modified steel was not suitable for use in shotgun barrels. He stated that the relatively high sulfur content permitted the formation of fatigue cracks, which eventually caused the barrel to fail under normal pressure loads. He also testified that Remington had thickened, and therefore strengthened, the barrel of the Model 1100 since the time Loitz's particular shotgun was produced. He based that opinion on measurements he obtained from more recently produced Model 1100 shotguns.

Vehemently disputing that claim, Remington presented testimony indicating that *no* change had been made in the thickness of the company's Model 1100 barrels. Remington also presented as an expert a professor of metallurgy from Lehigh University. He testified that the cause of the shotgun barrel explosion was a high-pressure shell. He based his conclusion on an examination of Loitz's gun in comparison to exemplar guns that had been intentionally exploded by the discharge of overloaded shells, as well as his own tests concerning the strength of AISI 1140 modified steel. From those tests, he concluded that the type of steel used by Remington was a safe and suitable material for the purpose it was designed and for the range of pressures it would normally be exposed to.

Remington also presented evidence that shotgun barrels can rupture or explode for a number of reasons unrelated to design or material composition. For example, a barrel might explode if obstructed with mud or ice. Also, in what is known as a "12-20 burst," a barrel might explode if a 12-gauge and a 20-gauge shell are discharged simultaneously, as when an unfired 20-gauge shell has been inadvertently left in the barrel. Remington witnesses testified that the sulfur content of the steel used by the company helps prevent fragmentation if a barrel does explode.

In addition, Remington presented testimony of a former executive of the company that had manufactured the reloading device used by the plaintiff. The witness described the machine and demonstrated its operation. Using the machine, he produced some overloaded shells, but he was unable to make a single shell that Remington suggested could have been the cause of the present accident.

At trial, the parties stipulated that mistakes can be made in the operation of a reloading machine, but they disputed the likelihood of producing, and not detecting, an overloaded shell, particularly one with more than twice the normal charge of gunpowder. Loitz's unused shells were recovered from the scene and tested. Remington conceded that the unused shells were not overloaded, and that, if fired, they would produce pressures within normal limits.

The parties stipulated that by the time of the plaintiff's accident, Remington had received notice of ninety-four other barrel explosions involving the Model 1100. In eighty-nine of the cases, the shooters claimed to have been using normal reloaded shells, while in the remaining five cases, the persons said they had used factory-made ammunition. In each of the ninety-four cases, however, Remington believed the explosion was caused by the use of a high-pressure shell.

Over Remington's objection, Loitz was permitted to present testimony of three individuals who had sustained personal injuries when the barrels of their Model 1100 shotguns exploded. The trial judge admitted the evidence only in relation to Loitz's claim for punitive damages and gave the jury limiting instructions to that effect.

The jury awarded Loitz $75,000 in compensatory damages and $1.6 million in punitive damages. The intermediate appellate court acknowledged that the amount of punitive damages awarded by the jury was large, but concluded that the case was appropriate for imposition of such damages.

The principal issue in the appeal to the Illinois Supreme Court concerned this imposition of $1.6 million in punitive damages, and Remington raised a number of challenges to the award. In advocating that punitive damages were appropriate, Loitz first referred to evidence showing that Remington knew of these ninety-four prior accidents involving Model 1100 shotguns. Remington presented testimony that the company had investigated each of those occurrences and had concluded in every case that the cause of the accident was a high-pressure shell, either reloaded or factory-loaded.

Remington also pointed out that the 94 prior accidents represented only about 0.003 percent of Remington's production of more than three million Model 1100 barrels. The prior accidents, Remington suggested, must be considered not only in relation to the number of barrels produced, but also in relation to the estimated number of times those guns would have been used. Thus, the prior explosions represented an extremely small percentage of Remington's production of gun barrels and an even smaller percentage of the number of times the shotguns were actually fired.

The Illinois Supreme Court did not consider the evidence sufficient to warrant imposition of punitive damages against Remington, regardless of whether the evidence was assessed under a standard of "flagrant indifference" to public safety or the more traditional "willful and wanton" misconduct. The court concluded that there was not sufficient proof that Remington had the requisite degree of culpability to warrant imposition of a sanction that was intended to punish and deter.

With the supreme court's decision firmly in hand, the Remington company continued on with production of the popular Model 1100—as they say in the business—full bore.

Hook & Bullet

Pursuit of the Wily Rabbit

Some hunters there are, of the super-refined and dudish sort, who deny to the rabbit any position among legitimate game animals; and there are others who, while grudgingly admitting rabbits to the list, seem to think it necessary to excuse their concession by calling them hares. I regard all this as pure affectation and nonsense. I deem it not beneath my dignity and standing as a reputable gunner to write of the rabbit as an entirely suitable member of the game community; and in doing so I am not dealing with hares or any other thing except plain, little every-day plebeian rabbits—sometimes appropriately called "cotton-tails." Though they may be "defamed by every charlatan" among hunters of self-constituted high degree, and despised by thousands who know nothing of their game qualities, I am not ashamed of their pursuit; and I count it by no means bad skill to force them by a successful shot to a topsy-turvy pause when at their best speed.

These sly little fellows feed at night, and during the day they hide so closely in grass or among rocks and brush that it is seldom they can be seen when at rest. Of course, no decent man will shoot a rabbit while sitting, and I have known them to refuse to start for anything less than a kick or punch. When they do start, however, they demonstrate quite clearly that they have kept their feet in the best possible position for a spring and run. After such a start the rabbit must in fairness be given an abundant chance to gain full headway, and when he has traversed the necessary distance for this, and is at his fastest gait, the hunter that shoots him has good reason to be satisfied with his marksmanship. I once actually poked one up and he escaped unhurt, though four loads of shot were sent after him.

In the main, however, dogs must be relied upon for the real enjoyment and success of rabbit hunting. The fastest dogs are not the best, because they are apt to chase the rabbit so swiftly and closely that he quickly betakes himself to a hole or other safe shelter, instead of relying upon his running ability. The baying of three or four good dogs steadily following a little cotton-tail should be as exhilarating and as pleasant to ears attuned to the music as if the chase were for bigger game. As the music is heard more distinctly, the hunter is allowed to flatter himself that his acute judgment can determine the route of the approaching game and the precise point from which an advantageous shot can be secured.

The self-satisfied conceit aroused by a fortunate guess concerning this important detail, especially if supplemented by a fatal shot, should permit the lucky gunner to enjoy as fully the complacent pleasurable persuasion that the entire achievement is due to his sagacity, keenness and skill as though the animal circumvented were a larger beast. In either case the hunter experiences the delight born of a well-fed sense of superiority and self-pride; and this, notwithstanding all attempts to keep it in the background, is the most gratifying factor in every sporting indulgence.

From *A Word Concerning Rabbit Hunting*, by Grover Cleveland (1905)

Chapter Five

Hunting Clothes:
Right to Use the Term "Safari"

Abercrombie & Fitch Co. v. Hunting World, Inc., 537 F.2d 4 (2d Cir. 1976)

Even in the non-hunting world, everyone is familiar with "safari clothes"—the jaunty African hunting-lodge attire such as the "safari hat," the broad, flat-brimmed hat with wide band, and the "safari jacket," the belted bush jacket with patch pockets and buttoned shoulder loops. This swashbuckling outfit also includes distinctive shirts, pants, belts, and boots, and these are typically khaki-colored.

Abercrombie & Fitch has long made a line of clothing in which it used registered trademarks for the word "Safari." The term fortuitously conveys to its affluent and globe-trotting patrons a romantic notion of high style, coupled with an attractive foreign allusion. When Abercrombie realized that a competing store known as Hunting World was likewise producing a line of such clothing, it immediately filed suit for trademark infringement.

Hunting World, the complaint alleged, had engaged in the retail marketing of sporting apparel (particularly hats and boots), which they identified using the term "Safari" alone or with such labels as "Minisafari" and "Safariland." Ambercrombie alleged that continuation of such infringement would confuse and deceive the public and thereby impair the distinct and unique quality of Ambercrombie‘s trademark. Hunting World countered that the word “safari” is an ordinary, common, descriptive, geographic, and generic word that is not capable of trademark protection.

Unfortunately for Ambercrombie, the district court not only dismissed the complaint, but canceled *all* of Ambercrombie’s “Safari” clothing registrations, including several that were not even in suit. The judge found that there was frequent use of the word “Safari” in connection with wearing apparel, that Ambercrobie’s policing efforts had obviously been unsuccessful, and that Ambercrombie had itself used the term in a descriptive sense not covered by its registration (for example, in urging customers to make a “Christmas Gift Safari” to their local Abercrombie & Fitch store).

The district court judge concluded that the term “Safari” was a very “weak” mark and one that was merely descriptive and did not serve to distinguish the plaintiff’s goods. Such terms are afforded protection by the Lanham Act only if they come to identify the *company* merchandising the product, rather than the product itself. The court held that Ambercrombie had failed to establish that this had become the situation with respect to the term “Safari.” The court entered a judgment dismissing the complaint and canceled not only the four registered trademarks in suit, but all Ambercrombie & Fitch’s other registered “Safari” trademarks.

Previous court decisions (and in some instances the Lanham Act itself) identify four categories of trademark protection. Arrayed in an ascending order roughly reflecting the degree of protection accorded, these classes are (1) generic, (2) descriptive, (3) suggestive, and (4) arbitrary or fanciful. The lines of demarcation, of course, are not always bright.

The difficulty of definition is compounded because a term

that is placed in one category for a particular product may be placed in quite a different category for another, because a term may (a) shift from one category to another in light of differences in usage through time, (b) have one meaning to one group of users and a different one to others, and (c) be put to different uses with respect to a single product. In various ways, all of these complications were involved in the instant case.

A generic term is one that refers to the genus of which the particular product is a species. At common law, neither those terms that were generic, nor those that were merely descriptive, could become valid trademarks. The same was true under the previous Trademark Act of 1905, except for marks that had been the subject of exclusive use for ten years prior to its enactment.

The Lanham Act made an important exception with respect to those merely descriptive terms that have acquired secondary meaning, but it offered no such exception for generic marks. The Act provided for the cancellation of a registered mark if at any time it became the common descriptive name of an article or substance. This meant that even proof of secondary meaning, by virtue of which some "merely descriptive" marks may be registered, cannot transform a generic term into a subject for trademark.

No matter how much money and effort the user of a generic term has poured into promoting the sale of its merchandise and no matter what success it has achieved in securing public identification, it cannot deprive competing manufacturers of the product of the right to call an article by its name.

The record abundantly supported the conclusion that many stores advertised "Safari" wearing apparel despite Abercrombie's attempts to police its mark. In contrast, the voluminous exhibits failed to disclose a single example of the use of "Safari" for boots by anyone other than Abercrombie & Fitch and Hunting World.

The court therefore noted that Abercrombie stood on stronger ground with respect to Hunting World's use of "Camel Safari," "Hippo Safari," and "Chukka Safari" as names for boots imported from Africa because there was no evidence that "Safari" had become a generic term for boots. Ambercrombie's registration of "Safari" for use on its boots had become incontestable, and it was immaterial whether Ambercrombie's use of "Safari" for boots was "suggestive" or "merely descriptive."

Hunting World contended, however, that even if "Safari"' was a valid trademark for boots, it was entitled to the defense of "fair use" within the Lanham Act. The Act offers such a defense even against marks that have become incontestable when the term alleged to be an infringement is not used as a trademark, but is instead used fairly and in good faith only to describe to users the goods or their geographic origin.

The parent company of Hunting World had engaged in arranging safaris to Africa since 1959. The president was the author of a book published in 1959 entitled *Safari Today*, and since 1961 had booked persons on safaris and purchased safari clothing in Africa for resale in America. These facts established that the defendant's use of "Safari" with respect to boots was made in the context of hunting expeditions and was not as an attempt to garner Abercrombie's goodwill.

The district court therefore found that Hunting World's use of "Camel Safari," "Hippo Safari," and "Safari Chukka" as names for various boots imported from Africa constituted a purely descriptive use to apprise the public of the type of product by referring to its origin and use.

On review, the Second Circuit reached the following conclusions:

(1) Applied to specific types of clothing, the term "Safari" had become a generic term.

(2) The name "Safari" had not, however, become a generic term for boots; it was either "suggestive" or "merely descriptive" and was a valid trademark, even if "merely descriptive," because it had become incontestable under the Lanham Act.

(3) The names "Camel Safari," "Hippo Safari," and "Safari Chukka" were devoted by Hunting World, which had a defense against a charge of infringement with respect to these on the basis of "fair use."

These are just a few tidbits to keep in mind the next time you happen to be on *safari*—to the shopping mall.

Hook & Bullet

Stalking the Mountain Goat

One day while out hunting I saw a big goat on a bluff off to my right and determined to try to get him for his head, which appeared through my telescope to be an unusually good one. He was about half a mile off when I first spied him and the bluff extended several miles to the southwest like a great wall shutting off the view in that direction. I worked up to the foot of the bluffs and then along; climbing up several hundred feet I struck a shelf which appeared to run along the face at about the height I had seen the goat. It was ticklish work, for the shelf was covered with slide rock which I had to avoid disturbing, and then, too, in places it dwindled to a ledge barely three feet wide with about five hundred feet of nothing underneath.

After about four hundred yards of this work I heard a rock fall above me and looking up saw the billy leaning over an outrageous corner looking at me. Aiming as nearly as I could straight up I let drive at the middle of the white mass. There was a grunt, a scramble and a lot of rocks, and then down came the goat, striking in between the cliff and a big boulder and not two feet from me. I fairly shivered for fear he would jump up and butt me off the ledge, but he only gave one quiver and lay still. The 330-grain bullet entering the stomach, had broken the spine and killed instantly. He was an old grandfather and had a splendid head, which I now treasure very highly. I took the head, skin, fat and some of the meat back to camp that night, having to pack it off the bluff in sections. The fat rendered out into three gold-pans full of lard. Goat-fat is excellent for frying and all through the trip it was a great saving on our bacon.

Then one night the snow came. We heard it gently tapping on the tent, and by morning there was three inches in our yard. The time had come only too soon to pull out, which we did about ten o'clock, bidding good-bye to our permanent camp with its comfortable windbreak, its fireplace, table and chairs. Below us

the river ran through a canon [canyon] and we had to cross quite a high mountain range to get through. As we ascended the snow got deeper and deeper. It was almost two feet deep on a level on top of the range. We had to go down a very steep hog-back, and here had trouble in plenty. The horses' feet balled up with snow and they were continually sliding. A pack horse slid down on top of my saddle horse and startled him. I was on foot in front and they knocked me down and the three of us slid until stopped by a fallen tree.

Such a mess I never saw. One horse was on top of another. The pack was loose and frozen ropes tangled up with everything. It took us half an hour to straighten up the mess and the frozen lash ropes cut our hands frightfully. My ankle had become slightly strained in the mix-up and for several days I suffered agonies with it. There was no stopping—we had to hit the trail hard or get snowed in. One day we stopped to hunt. Bill went out while I nursed my leg. He brought in a fine seven-point buck.

Speaking of the hunt he said: "I jumped the buck in a flat of down timber. He was going like mad about a hundred yards off

Hook & Bullet (continued)

when I first spied him. I threw up the old rifle and blazed away five times before he tumbled. Each time I pulled I was conscious that the sights looked just like that trademark of the Lyman sight showing the running deer and the sight. When I went over to look at the buck I had a nice little bunch of five shots right behind the shoulder. Those Lyman sights are surely the sights for a hunting rifle." Bill was one of the best shots on game I ever saw. One day I saw him cut the heads off of three grouse in trees while he sat in the saddle with his horse walking up hill. Both our rifles did mighty good work. The more I use a rifle the more I become convinced of the truth of the saying, "Beware of the man with one gun." Get a good rifle to suit you exactly. Fix the trigger pull and sights exactly as you wish them and then stick to that gun as long as it will shoot accurately and you will make few misses in the field.

Only too soon we drove our pack-train into the post. As we rode up two men were building a shack. One of them dropped a board and we nearly jumped out of our skins at the terrific noise. My! How loud everything sounded to our ears, accustomed only to the stillness of those grand mountains. We stayed at the post three days, disposing of our horses and boxing up our heads and skins, and then pulled out for civilization. Never again will such experiences come to us. The day of the wilderness hunter has gone for good. And so the hunt of our lives came to an end.

From *Red Letter Days in British Columbia*, by Townsen Whelen (1901)

Chapter Six

Fishing Rod Wars:
Can Green Poles be Trademarked?

R.L. Winston Rod Co. v. Sage Manufacturing Co., 838 F. Supp. 1396 (Mont. 1993)

The R.L. Winston Rod Company began manufacturing fly-fishing rods in 1929. The company was founded in California, but later moved its operations to Twin Bridges, Montana—not far from the renowned headwaters of the Missouri River.

Winston makes expensive rods of both traditional bamboo and more modern materials. In the 1970s, space-age technology brought the advent of graphite, and Winston began selling those hi-tech rods in the now-familiar color of green.

Defendants Sage Manufacturing and Orvis Services likewise manufacture graphite fly rods in competition with Winston. Winston sought a preliminary injunction enjoining Sage and Orvis from selling expensive graphite rods in any shade of the color green. It claimed that it was the first to use the color, that it has featured green in its advertising and promotions, and that its rods had become known to the public as "the green rod." Winston alleged that the defendants introduced their green rods into the market fifteen years later and thereby violated various state trade practice acts by diluting the trademark.

The defendants moved to dismiss on the ground that a color is not entitled to trademark protection.

Although Winston's suit seemed facially directed at all green fly-fishing rods, the company claimed that it was not directed at any but "high-end green graphite rods,“ particularly those costing more than $350. This meant that green graphite fishing rods sold by L.L.Bean and Cabela's at prices below that amount did not fall within the protected class. This apparently narrowed the field to two manufacturers other than Winston who also offered green graphite rods—Sage and Orvis.

It was Sage's testimony that if money were no object, one could not produce a finer rod than Sage's flagship model, which retailed at about $500. The Orvis line likewise indicated an upper price level near $500. Thus, Winston's case was directed only at green graphite fly-fishing rods selling at retail prices ranging from approximately $350 to a $500 and manufactured by Sage or Orvis.

Winston brought its claim under the anti-dilution statutes of eight states. Under these statutes, an injunction could be granted where the first user showed that the mark was distinctive and the subsequent user's application of that mark diluted its distinctiveness. To prevail on the merits, Winston had to prove it was entitled to trademark protection in the color green as used in high-end graphite fly rods.

The court first remarked that state unfair competition laws were designed to promote ethical business practices. If a business finds a successful method of marketing its products, other businesses may not unfairly capitalize on it. Of course, not all marketing methods are protected. To secure exclusive use of a trademark, the claimant must establish that the mark is distinctive or that it has acquired a "secondary meaning," that is, that consumers associate the mark with the goods. Trademark registration serves these functions; in the absence of registration, the claimant must prove them.

Sage and Orvis claimed that even if Winston established its claim to the color green, the claim must fail as a matter of law because historically, color alone has not been protected by trademark. While this is true, the court noted that the trend has been toward protection. In a landmark case involving fiberglass insulation manufactured by Owens-Corning, the court permitted registration of the color pink as a trademark for the manufacturer's residential insulation. But color is not always entitled to protection as a mark, and the facts and circumstances of each case must be examined.

As for all marks, compliance with the legal requirements for registration depends on the particular mark and its circumstances of use. In determining the potentiality for registration of color marks, courts have considered factors such as the nature of the goods, how the color is used, the range of colors or color combinations available, the number of competitors, and customary marketing practices.

Earlier decisions evidenced a concern that permitting a trademark in a color would restrict competition because there are only a limited number of colors in the palette. The court in the Owens-Corning case dealt a blow to this "color depletion theory" when it found that even if Owens-Corning were given exclusive use of the color pink for fiberglass insulation, all other shades of color would still be available to other manufacturers. Therefore, competition would not be hindered by reserving exclusive use of the color pink to one manufacturer.

In contrast to the many shades of color available for fiberglass insulation, the evidence showed that the color palette available for the manufacture of fly rods was extremely limited. One limiting factor was the method by which the color was applied to the rod. Graphite is a carbon, and so it is naturally black. The color must be applied as a dye, not a paint. Only a few dark shades successfully mask the black base, and colors applied to it darken deeply. Under these circumstances, granting exclusive use of a color to one manufacturer would severely restrict competition; there would be little left for the rest of the world.

A second reason for denying trademark protection to a color arises when the color serves a functional purpose. One functional purpose is utilitarian functionality, where the color has a meaningful significance. For example, one court held that the Sylvania "Blue Dot" on a flashbulb could not be the subject of trademark registration because blue served the utilitarian function of indicating air leakage. Another functional purpose is aesthetic functionality, where the color gives a manufacturer an advantage because the consumer deems the particular color to be more attractive for that type of item.

If the particular feature is an important ingredient in the commercial success of the product, the interest in competition permits its imitation in the absence of a patent or copyright. On the other hand, where the design is a mere arbitrary embellishment, and hence unrelated to basic consumer demands in connection with the product, imitation may be forbidden where the requisite showing of secondary meaning is made.

Sage and Orvis, the court said, had not shown that the color green in a fly rod served any utilitarian function. The color came closer to serving an aesthetic function. The evidence indicated that consumers of high-end fly rods preferred rods in a limited range of colors, principally those that evoke the natural colors of the outdoor environment in which they are used—for example, green, black, and brown. It is not as important to categorize the function of the color, however, as it is to determine whether manufacturers had a competitive reason for using a limited number of colors. If competitive factors restrict the available colors, then color may be functional.

The court found that Sage and Orvis had proven that the range of available colors was limited. In the Owens-Corning case, the court found that because there was no limitation on the colors available for fiberglass insulation, the color pink was entirely arbitrary and served no functional purpose. Furthermore, the color of the fiberglass insulation is concealed when the product is installed. But with graphite fly rods, the palette was limited by the dyeing process and by consumer preference. Moreover, Winston sought exclusive use of *all* shades of green. Under these circumstances, the court noted that recognition of the trademark would considerably reduce competition in an unacceptable manner.

A trademark is distinctive when it identifies the particular source of the product or distinguishes it from other products. Correspondingly, a product's trademark acquires a secondary meaning when the public associates the mark with a single producer rather than the product itself.

The green in a fly rod is not inherently distinctive, like the words "Kodak" or "Xerox." It does not by itself indicate the source of the product. Winston therefore had to show that its mark had acquired a secondary meaning—the public association of Winston with that particular color.

Winston argued that it was widely known as "the green fly rod." However, the evidence at best showed that this meant that all Winston graphite fly rods were green, *not* that the public perceived that all green fly rods were made by Winston. The evidence casted (no pun intended) considerable doubt on Winston's allegation that it was the sole manufacturer of green graphite fly-rods. In fact, the weight of the evidence was to the contrary.

Furthermore, Winston had not promoted this alleged distinctive quality. The company introduced considerable evidence, including fishing catalogs, in which third parties had alluded to the green color of Winston rods. But lacking was substantial evidence that Winston itself promoted this color as a distinctive feature. Other than the instant lawsuit, Winston had not taken any overt action to protect its rights or enforce its claim. This lack of action was contrasted with Owens-Corning's substantial efforts to advertise its pink insulation in order to reinforce the secondary meaning in the eyes of the public.

To establish secondary meaning, Winston offered the results of a survey. However, the survey solicited the views of sellers of the product, not the consuming public. The court noted that the survey was questionable at best. Even if taken at face value, it did not establish that Winston has created a secondary meaning. Winston identified a number of manufacturers of high-end green fishing rods, including some not parties to this lawsuit. Winston interpreted this result as evidence of successful dilution by Orvis and Sage.

The court surmised that Winston could not have it both ways. If all the responses to the survey had mentioned Winston, the company would have argued that it had established *secondary meaning*; if no response had mentioned Winston, the company would have argued that it had established *dilution*.

The appellate court acknowledged that while there are circumstances in which a color is entitled to trademark protection, Winston would likely not prevail in its attempts. The court denied Winston's request for a preliminary injunction.

In doing so, the court, at least for the time being, perpetuated the brisk competition by Sage and Orvis to Winston's venerable "green machine."

Hook & Bullet

Dreams of an Angler

A few years ago I found my domicile in famed Sleepy Hollow, near Tarrytown. The little brook that passed my door leaped into the Pocantico nearby the rock whereon the oldest inhabitant averred that Irving sat and fished. It was an ideal spot to lure a dreamer. The living waters of three brooks met and mingled. Well, indeed, might this spot be hallowed in the memory by the legend, which recalls the brook "with just murmur enough to lure one to repose," hard by the then old schoolhouse.

In an idle moment, I, too, sat upon that rock, with, by chance, rod and line. A quiet, cool, refreshing spot, indeed. A limpid pool below formed near an old wall, over which a wooden bridge was thrown. Swirling bubbles gathered, lingered, and then strung off as the ripples danced along. Overhanging branches nearly touched the water, and vines trailed along the banks. By no special direction my line floated down to this spot. In a lazy, listless way I drew the line back too quickly. I had unconsciously perpetrated a skilful play. A sturdy fish rose to seize the bait. I saw the white belly and sudden splash. My former experience gave me to understand that I had lost a beautiful trout. I was not long in solving the secret.

By cautious lingerings I lured many trout. Knowledge came with experience, and day by day I took practice lessons at my door. With confidence and courage I ventured to adjacent streams and favorite pools, always with success, when the strictest caution was observed. I studied the habits of the trout and lured him with every variety of seasonable bait and color. I was loth to deceive the noble trout with artificial fly, preferring the natural variety, but occasionally added a bit of color, which may have appealed to a passion other than that of gluttony.

From *The Sportsman Tourist*, by John A. Lant (1900)

Chapter Seven

Safety Orange:
Impingements on Freedom of Religion

State v. Bontrager, 683 N.E.2d 126 (Ohio 1996)

In late November a sportsman named Adam Bontrager was deer hunting on his father's farmland in northwest Ohio. He was not, as required by state law, wearing a hunter-orange hat, vest, or jacket.

Bontrager was a devoted member of the Old Order Amish faith, and he claimed that wearing such vivid clothing would cause him to violate his religious beliefs. The municipal court nevertheless found him guilty of violating the law and fined him accordingly.

Bontrager filed an appeal, asserting that the state law violated his rights to free exercise of religion under both federal and state constitutions. The standard by which the appellate court reviewed this hunting regulation was the tripartite test enunciated by the United States Supreme Court and later adopted by the Ohio Supreme Court.

This test consists of first, whether a defendant's religious beliefs are sincerely held; second, whether the regulation infringes upon a defendant's constitutional right to freely engage in religious practices; and third, whether the state has demonstrated a compelling interest for enforcement of the regulation

and whether the regulation is written in the least restrictive means.

The test to ascertain the sincerity of Bontrager‘s religious beliefs was whether “a given belief that is sincere and meaningful occupies a place in the life of its possessor parallel to that filled by the orthodox belief in God.” Although this is an encompassing definition, satisfaction requires more than a personal or philosophical belief. The belief at issue here was that the Amish must be separate from this world, not associate with nonbelievers, remain self-sufficient, and exist without the intrusion of, or reliance on, the outside world.

What most people view as necessities—cars, indoor plumbing, phones, electricity, and other modern conveniences—are disregarded by the Amish. Another example of this separateness is the Amish practice of refraining from fashionable or brightly colored clothing in favor of the more subdued navy or black. Bontrager was a practicing member of the Amish religion, and he maintained that the wearing of bright colors could lead to sanctions imposed by the church. The court never questioned the sincerity of Bontrager's religious belief.

Previous decisions are clear that free exercise of religion has been impaired when one is forced to choose between following the precepts of a religion and forfeiting governmental benefits, on one hand, and abandoning one of the precepts of the religion in order to accept government benefits, on the other. In other words, government cannot condition benefits or privileges on conduct that causes an individual to violate his religious beliefs.

In this case, hunting is clearly a government-sponsored benefit. It occurs only according to legislative grant: wild animals are considered to be owned by the state in trust for the benefit of the public, and they may be hunted only with legislative permission. As such, hunting is a privilege for which the legislature may prescribe certain terms and conditions.

Hunting is not a central tenet of the Amish religion. Nothing in the defendant's religion compelled him to hunt deer. For the Amish, hunting is an aid to the belief of self-sufficiency, but is not the prescribed method to fulfill this principle. Other activities can also serve to satisfy this doctrine, such as farming, raising livestock, and bartering for goods. Other food sources besides deer were necessary to sustain Bontrager's family, since hunting regulations allowed killing only three deer a year.

The court noted too that sufficient accommodations existed within the game regulations to allow the Amish to hunt without wearing hunter orange. For example, hunter orange was required only for the deer-hunting primitive weapons, statewide primitive weapons, and deer gun-hunting seasons. The remainder of the deer-hunting season—the three and a half months from the first Saturday in October to the following January 31—was devoted to longbow and crossbow hunting, in which hunter orange need not be worn. Thus, the defendant could hunt deer with either a longbow or a crossbow for a majority of the hunting season without the need to claim a religious exemption from the hunter-orange requirement.

Furthermore, all other animals may be hunted without the hunter-orange requirement. The regulation at issue applied only to the deer gun-hunting and primitive-weapons seasons. The only other time hunter orange was required was during the statewide primitive weapons season, when only deer, waterfowl, and coyotes may be hunted. Otherwise, any animal may be hunted with a gun during the appropriate season without invoking the requirement. Bontrager could therefore hunt game birds, furbearing animals, and wild turkeys during their respective hunting seasons. As a result, the court concluded that the requirement did not place an undue burden on the defendant's religious practices.

The court noted that the state clearly had compelling interests that were inherent to its police powers and superior to Bontrager's claim of freedom from the requirement. The state's use of police powers are held valid when the regulation bears a real and substantial relation to public health, safety, morals, or general welfare.

The hunter-orange regulation was deemed to be a valid form of firearms control. The reasoning for upholding the requirement is similar to that of seat-belt requirements. Seat belt requirements often save drivers' lives, improve the safety of other drivers on the road, and reduce the impact of accidents on taxpayers because of the lesser need for long-term care. Like automobile accidents, gun-hunting accidents can have life-threatening ramifications. Allowing Bontrager to hunt without wearing safety orange placed him at risk of being shot by another hunter. Alternately, Bontrager risked accidentally shooting another person.

Bontrager's constitutional claim was therefore rejected because, although he sincerely held his religious beliefs, the regulation did not infringe upon his religious practices, and the state had compelling interests in regulating firearms.

In the end, one wonders whether, as a result of this case, the hills of Ohio are now full of florescent Amish hunters, secretly resenting not only the power of the state—but clothing in an obnoxious shade of orange.

Hook & Bullet

Tale of a Tiger

I shot my first tiger in the Kanker State in the Central Provinces in January, 1900, under the wing of a gentleman who had shot many tigers and had had much experience of the sport. The lesson, which I had taken most to heart, was that a long shot taken in the direction of the beat [group of tigers] might drive the tiger back into the beat and lead to a casualty among the beaters.

There were three tigers in the beat, a tigress and two three-quarter grown cubs. My machan [tree platform] had been tied in front so as to give me the first chance of a shot, and my mentor sat in a machan behind me, so as to shoot any animal which might escape me. My machan was badly tied, especially for a man shooting, as I do, from the left shoulder. The string bed,

which formed it, was tied with one end facing the beat, and along the left of the machan there were tree trunks. On this side, therefore, I could fire only straight in front of me, but I was too inexperienced to recognize fully the unsatisfactory nature of the position, and settled myself in the machan without making any objection.

As the beat proceeded the tigress appeared and stood on my left front, looking up apparently at one of the stops. She gave me as good a shot as I have ever had in a beat, as she was broadside on and quite motionless; but the distance was over 100 yards, and, being very anxious not to be the cause of any mishap, I decided to allow her to approach. Suddenly, with a "wouf," she started off at a gallop to the left, passed instantly out of my fire zone, and I was compelled to look on helplessly as she passed the machan. She was fired at but missed by my mentor, and got clean away. One of the cubs followed, and I got in a shot at it, as it passed, but missed. The other cub gave me an easy shot, and I killed it. If I had shot the tigress we should probably have bagged all three, but I had correctly carried out instructions, and the instructions were absolutely sound. The line between success and failure, in big-game shooting, is a very narrow one.

I then shot a fine tiger in a beat in the Bustar State, killing him with a single shot as he walked fast through the bushes. I also killed a fine panther by moonlight, when sitting up over a kill, though the body was unfortunately not found until the skin was spoiled. On the whole, therefore, I did pretty well for a beginner in this expedition.

From *Some Tiger Stories*, by Richard Dane (1901)

Chapter Eight

Illegal Fishing Devices:

Playing by the Rules

Willaby v. State, 698 S.W.2d 473 (Tex. App. 1985)

Early one morning in June, a Texan named Kendall Kinslow was fishing at Lake Tawakoni, and he had chosen a popular fishing spot known affectionately to the locals as "the levee."

Kinslow observed two individuals—John Willaby and David Breding—walk past him carrying a "noodling pole,“ which is an unusual device used to *snag* fish rather than catch them in the traditional way. Willaby and Breding also carried a lantern and a dip net. Kinslow watched Willaby wade deeply into the water with the noodling pole and snag catfish among the rocks, while Breding collected them in a dip net.

Noodling poles are specifically declared to be illegal fishing devices under Texas law. Sensing his civic obligation to report this violation, Kinslow promptly proceeded to call the game warden. The officer arrived, and from a concealed spot behind several trees, he observed Willaby and Breding working with the noodling pole and dip net. The area was well lit by a lantern.

After observing the scene for about twenty minutes, the game warden arrested the two men as they were leaving the water. The officer confiscated the noodling pole, dip net, and catfish, and these items were stored at his home until trial when they were admitted into evidence.

Willaby and Breding were charged with violation of the Texas law that specifically provides: "It is unlawful to use a hand-operated device under water designed to snag fish, commonly called 'noodling' poles or gaffs." Willaby and Breding were subsequently convicted of the offense in justice court. They appealed and received a trial *de novo* in the county court, which found them guilty of the same charge and assessed each of the men a fine of $118.50.

Never before in the history of fish-and-game litigation has anyone worked harder to overturn a fine of $118.50. Willaby and Breding appealed their conviction, and in doing so, they advanced three grounds for reversal: (1) the evidence was insufficient to sustain a conviction, (2) the proper chain of custody was not used to preserve the physical evidence, and (3) the statute upon which the convictions were based was too vague to be enforceable.

The appellate court, however, found the evidence clearly adequate to support the appellants' convictions. Several witnesses testified that Breding carried the dip net into the water as Willaby carried the noodling pole, and that Breding was plainly seen using the dip net to land catfish hooked by Willaby.

Willaby and Breding also complained about admission into evidence of the noodling pole, dip net, and catfish seized at the time of their arrest. The game warden testified that after the arrest he placed the noodling pole in the attic of his home. Although the pole was not under lock and key, only the game warden and his wife had access to the attic.

The game warden also testified he seized the catfish from Breding at the time of his arrest, and that he immediately placed them in Willaby's ice chest until he arrived at his home, where he tagged the fish, placed them in a sack, and then stored the sack in the freezer in his garage. The garage was attached to the house and both doors were locked when the game warden and his wife were not present. The fish were removed from the freezer and the pole removed from the attic only for use in court. The court concluded that the evidence was sufficiently secured for introduction at trial.

In a last-gasp effort at reversing his conviction, Willaby suggested that the hook he used was baited with rubber worms, and thus he had *invented* a new kind of fishing not prohibited by state law. He claimed his new fishing method was to thread the end of the worm onto the barbs of the treble hook in a manner that the barbs would be covered. Willaby denied that the hook could be used to snag fish. He admitted (a) that there was in fact no worm on his hook at the time of his arrest and (b) that to use this new method of fishing, it would be necessary to hold the entire device under water.

The appellate court immediately rejected Willaby's contention that there was no law in effect to prohibit his "new" method of fishing. Without further discussion of the issue of an artificial lure, the court found that because Willaby's entire device—baited or unbaited—must be held under water, it would sustain a conviction for violation of the statute.

As a result, Willaby and Breding were each poorer in the sum of $118.50. And with the confiscation of their fishing weapons now officially confirmed, the two Texans, it seemed certain, would noodle no more.

Hook & Bullet

A Day at the Lake

It had been a delicious afternoon on Profile Lake; one of those days when the very glory of the other country seems to come down among our mountains. The little lake had presented, as usual on such evenings, a gay and brilliant scene. It was a lake of Paradise. A dozen boats were out with parties of ladies or with anglers, some of the latter fishing with floats and worms, some casting flies, and now and then getting up fair trout. I had passed the time after a fashion that is somewhat lazy and luxurious, lying at full length in the bottom of my boat, drifting idly around while I read an old book, occasionally sinking into a doze and dreaming. As evening came down the various parties left the lake, and at last in the twilight Dupont came up in his boat alongside of mine, and we found ourselves, as often before, alone on the lake.

Among all my memories of trout fishing there are none more pleasant than the memories of those evenings on Profile Lake, when my friend and I, with our boats at anchor a few rods apart, have cast our flies long after the darkness prevented our seeing their fall, and whether we got rises or not were content to see the stars come over the mountains, or the moonlight descend into the ravine and silver the surface of the lake.

This evening was profoundly still; not a breath of air disturbed the leaf of a tree. One could hardly hope to find a Profile Lake trout so foolish as to take a fly on such a glassy surface. I was lazy and indolent, but Dupont was making long and steady casts, always graceful, and as sure as graceful. I paused and watched him. I could just see in the twilight the fall of his tail fly, some fifty feet away from his hand, as it touched the water close inshore under a great rock, and I felt in my own arm the thrill which was in his as I saw the slightest commotion on the surface, and knew that a good fish had risen and "sucked in" the fly without striking it. It was a very pretty contest then, with his light Norris rod and a fish that would weigh over a pound.

The silence was profound. No sound on water or land or in the air. Few night birds are heard in our forests thereabouts, and in the cool evenings the insects are still. So I looked on while he patiently wearied and landed his fish—a good size for this overfished lake, where the trout have little chance to grow large. It is in some respects the most wonderful trout pond I have ever known.

From *Three Bottles of Claret*, by W.C. Prime (1888)

Chapter Nine

Shot While Jogging:
Failure of the City to Protect

Elliott v. Waterbury, 715 A.2d 27 (Conn. 1998)

Kevin Elliott was jogging on Pitch Road, an unpaved lane near the towns of Morris and Waterbury, Connecticut, when he was accidentally shot and killed by a hunter.

The shooter, Robert Cook, was hunting in the 1800-acre watershed area adjacent to the road and on property owned by the city. Pitch Road was snow-plowed by the town of Morris so that Waterbury workers could daily read the instruments at the reservoir. The road was also used by walkers, joggers, and hunters who travelled it to gain access to the watershed area.

Elliott's widow filed a wrongful death action against the Waterbury and Morris municipalities, claiming in essence that the municipalities and their employees (1) were willfully, intentionally, and maliciously negligent by allowing hunting on the watershed property and by failing to take steps to make the activity safe, and (2) acted wantonly and recklessly by failing to take appropriate steps to alleviate the danger posed to pedestrians by the hunting on the watershed property, despite actual knowledge of that danger.

The trial court concluded that, given the intervening role of the hunter in causing the decedent's death, the municipal defendants were shielded from liability by a statute recognizing that municipalities cannot be held liable for acts or omissions of persons other than their employees, officers, or agents. The court rendered summary judgment in favor of the defendants, from which Jean Elliott, the administratrix of the estate of Kevin Elliott, appealed.

The principal issue in the appeal was whether the Connecticut statute established a sole proximate causation standard—or some other heightened causation standard—in order to establish the tort liability of a municipality or its employees, officers, or agents.

The trial court concluded that the statute established either (a) a rule that in order for a municipality or its agents, officers, or employees to be held liable, a person must be injured solely and proximately from the acts or omissions of the municipality, or (b) a rule that the municipality's negligence be the direct cause of the injury and not that of a third party.

Given the role of the hunter in causing the death of the decedent, the appellate court concluded that the statute provided immunity from liability for the municipal defendants, regardless of which of these two rules the subsection is thought to embody.

In the appeal, the plaintiff claimed that the trial court improperly interpreted the statute. She argued that the provision should not be interpreted as incorporating "a sole proximate cause" standard or a "direct cause" standard because either rule would represent a dramatic shift away from the common-law standards concerning causality in tort actions against municipalities or their employees, without a clear indication of such a legislative intention in the text of the statute or its legislative history.

The appellate court concluded, however, that the statute

should not be interpreted as establishing a causation standard based on either the concept of the primary causation or the concept of the most immediate causation. First, there was no clear indication in either the language or the legislative history that the legislature intended either such meaning. Moreover, both a causation standard based on chronological immediacy and one based on relative proportion of causation, like a sole proximate causation rule, would shield municipal defendants from liability in many negligent supervision actions.

Either standard would conflict with the legislature's clear intent in enacting the Tort Reform Act of 1986, *not* to provide any additional immunity to municipal defendants beyond that provided already by the doctrine of governmental immunity.

Most importantly, reading these concepts into the statute would violate the principle that courts generally will not interpret a statute as effecting a change in a fundamental common-law principle—specifically the rule that the ordinary proximate causation standard applies to most tort actions against municipalities—in the absence of a clear indication of legislative intent to do so.

The court warned that to read either of these concepts into the statute would require changing fundamental principles of the common law in the name of statutory interpretation, but with no guidance from the statutory language or legislative history as to the shape of the new rule, nor even any clear suggestion that such a rule was intended. This the court declined to do.

The plaintiff claimed that the alleged conduct did not constitute a governmental act because it concerned a proprietary, as opposed to a public, activity, namely, the operation of a water utility. In support of her claim, the plaintiff relied upon three cases involving negligence actions arising out of a municipality's operation of a water utility. In each of those cases, the court held that the municipal defendants could not avail themselves of immuni-

ty because the municipalities engaged in the allegedly tortuous actions for the sake of corporate gain rather than for the administration of government. The present court concluded, however, that those cases were inapplicable to the present case.

In the instant case, the Waterbury defendants' allegedly tortious conduct—opening the watershed land to hunting and the manner in which it regulated that activity—was unrelated to its operation of a water utility. The plaintiff never revealed such a connection. It was apparent, instead, that that activity consisted of a set of policy decisions—which the plaintiff conceded required the exercise of judgment and discretion—concerning the use of city land for recreational purposes.

Moreover, the plaintiff did not allege, nor was there any indication in the record, that Waterbury received corporate gain or benefit from the hunting. Under these circumstances, the court concluded that, as a matter of law, the conduct the plaintiff complained of constituted governmental, not proprietary, acts.

In light of the fact that the tract was 1800 acres in size and that no municipal ordinance barred hunting on it; in light of the statutory and financial support of the state in maintaining hunting for recreation and wildlife management; and in light of the existence of a state regulatory regime that was designed to regulate hunting safety, the court concluded that the plaintiff's evidence was insufficient to establish wanton, reckless, willful, intentional, or malicious conduct.

The evidence simply did not provide a basis upon which a trier of fact could reasonably find that any acts of the city reached the level of "highly unreasonable conduct, involving an extreme departure from ordinary care, in a situation where a high degree of danger is apparent."

The court therefore confirmed that the law of sovereign immunity is still very much intact in the state of Connecticut, and that joggers on public lands best be on the lookout for hunters with loaded guns.

Hook & Bullet

The African Safari

On July 24th, in order to ship our fresh accumulations of specimens and trophies, we once more went into Nairobi. It was a pleasure again to see its tree-bordered streets and charming houses bowered in vines and bushes, and to meet once more the men and women who dwelt in the houses. I wish it were in my power to thank individually the members of the many East African households of which I shall always cherish warm memories of friendship and regard.

At Nairobi I saw Selous, who had just returned from a two months' safari with McMillan, Williams, and Judd. Their experience shows how large the element of luck is in lion hunting. Selous was particularly anxious to kill a good lion; there is nowhere to be found a more skilful or more hardworking hunter; yet he never even got a shot. Williams, on the other hand, came across three. Two he killed easily. The third charged him. He was carrying a double-barreled .450, but failed to stop the beast; it seized him by the leg, and his life was saved by his Swahili gun-bearer, who gave the lion a fatal shot as it stood over him. He came within an ace of dying; but when I saw him, at the hospital, he was well on the road to recovery.

One day Selous while on horseback saw a couple of lionesses, and galloped after them, followed by Judd, seventy or eighty yards behind. One lioness stopped and crouched under a bush, let Selous pass, and then charged Judd. She was right alongside him, and he fired from the hip; the bullet went into her eye; his horse jumped and swerved at the shot, throwing him off, and he found himself sitting on the ground, not three yards from the dead lioness. Nothing more was seen of the other.

Continually I met men with experiences in their past lives which showed how close the country was to those primitive conditions in which warfare with wild beasts was one of the main features of man's existence. At one dinner my host and two of my fellow-guests had been within a year or eighteen months severely mauled by lions. All three, by the way, informed me that the actual biting caused them at the moment no pain whatever; the pain came later. On meeting Harold Hill, my companion on one of my Kapiti Plains lion hunts, I found that since I had seen him he had been roughly handled by a dying leopard. The government had just been obliged to close one of the trade routes to native caravans because of the ravages of a man-eating lion, which carried men away from the camps. A safari which had come in from the north had been charged by a rhino, and one of the porters tossed and killed, the horn being driven clear through his loins.

From *Elephant Hunting on Mount Kenya*, by Theodore Roosevelt (1910)

Chapter Ten

An Accidental Fish Hook in the Eye:

Assumption of the Risk

Hawayek v. Simmons, 91 So.2d 49 (La. App. 1956)

On a fine April day, William Simmons and his brother-in-law, Alberto Hawayek, were fishing from an 18-foot-long open boat propelled by an outboard motor. They were cruising Louisiana's Lake Pontchartrain near what is fondly known to the local anglers as "Hospital Foundation."

Simmons was casting a relatively short five-foot rod with a deadly lure—one that incorporated a *triple* fishhook on the end. After making an overhand cast, he felt his lure strike an obstruction of some kind, and looking around, he discovered that his fish hook had unfortunately struck Hawayek in the right eye and then lodged firmly in his cheek.

Hawayek was immediately rushed to a clinic at Slidell, Louisiana, where physicians administered medication to alleviate his pain and suffering, before he was taken to a hospital in New Orleans. He was hospitalized for five days, and for three more weeks it was necessary for him to keep his eye bandaged. Fortuitously, he completely recovered his vision.

Hawayek brought this suit against Simmons and his liability

insurer in the sum of $21,104 for personal injuries, medical expenses, and other damages. His petition alleged that the defendant was negligent in several respects. The defendant responded there was no fault or negligence on his part, and in the alternative, claimed that by going fishing, plaintiff assumed the related risks.

The evidence revealed that just prior to the moment the defendant's lure struck him in the eye, the plaintiff was seated in the bow of the boat with his head down and looking into the water. The plaintiff stated that he did not see the lure coming toward his face. He suddenly felt a stinging sensation in his eye and then extracted the hook. The defendant could not explain any of his actions, nor did he deny negligence.

After a trial on the merits, there was rendered judgment in favor of the plaintiff for the sum of $154.65, representing medical and hospital expenses. The trial court was of the opinion that the amount was due to plaintiff under the defendant's insurance policy without regard to any negligence on the part of the defendant. However, the judge disallowed all other claims because he felt the plaintiff had not proven any negligence.

The plaintiff appealed the trial court's judgment. The appellate court held that under these circumstances the doctrine of *res ipsa loquitur* was applicable. In cases where (a) the plaintiff cannot be expected to have any information about the causes of the accident, (b) the defendant must be assumed to be fully informed on the subject, and (c) the accident is of the kind which ordinarily does not occur when due care has been exercised, the rule of evidence states that the accident speaks for itself—*res ipsa loquitur*.

In such cases, the plaintiff need not allege the particular acts of omission or commission from which the accident has resulted, much less prove them. As a result of the doctrine, there arises the legal presumption of superior knowledge on the part of the owner, possessor, or operator of the instrumentality which caused the injury.

In the case at bar, the plaintiff's attention was directed to a fish alongside the boat when the defendant's lure struck him in the eye. He was not looking at the defendant, so it was impossible for him to say exactly what might have caused the accident. The court assumed, however, that the defendant was fully informed as to what caused the lure to damage the plaintiff's eye. The court noted that when a fisherman makes an overhead-forward cast, his lure would not be expected to take a tangent that would strike another person in the boat, unless there was some fault or negligence on the part of the one who made the cast.

The court concluded that since the defendant failed to show he was free from negligence, then the defendant, who had sole charge of the instrumentality that caused the injury to plaintiff—that is, the fishing rod and triple fish hook—was presumed negligent from the occurrence of the accident itself.

The appellate court then turned to the defendant's contention that there can be no recovery because the plaintiff assumed all incidental risks of such a fishing expedition, including the risk of injury from an accident such as the one that occurred. The court concluded that while it might be said that one who becomes part of a fishing venture assumes all *ordinary* and *normal* hazards incident to the sport, the law does not require him to assume *all* risks of negligence of others in the fishing party. Hawayek and Simmons were the only occupants of the boat, and there is no valid reason why the plaintiff should have foreseen that the defendant would cast his line horizontally into the boat so that the lure would cause injury to him.

Taking into consideration the nature of the plaintiff's injury, his stay in the hospital, the necessity of having the eye bandaged for four weeks, and the physical pain and suffering and mental anguish, the appellate court maintained that the amount of the award should be increased by $1,500. The court therefore awarded the plaintiff the sum of $1,654.65.

More than anything else, this decision confirms the fact that fishing can be a riskier pursuit than one might expect. And those who engage in it are best advised to wear a protective helmet and goggles.

Hook & Bullet

Wary Prey

The neighborhood of Streatley and Goring is a great fishing center. There is some excellent fishing to be had here. The river abounds in pike, roach, dace, gudgeon, and eels, just here; and you can sit and fish for them all day.

Some people do. They never catch them. I never knew anybody catch anything, up the Thames, except minnows and dead cats, but that has nothing to do, of course, with fishing! The local fisherman's guide doesn't say a word about catching anything. All it says is the place is "a good station for fishing"; and, from what I have seen of the district, I am quite prepared to bear out this statement.

There is no spot in the world where you can get more fishing, or where you can fish for a longer period. Some fishermen come here and fish for a day, and others stop and fish for a month. You can hang on and fish for a year, if you want to: it will be all the same.

The *Angler's Guide to the Thames* says that "jack and perch are also to be had about here," but there the *Angler's Guide* is wrong. Jack and perch may be about there. Indeed, I know for a fact that they are. You can see them there in shoals, when you are out for a walk along the banks: they come and stand half out of the water with their mouths open for biscuits. And, if you go for a bathe, they crowd round, and get in your way, and irritate you. But they are not to be "had" by a bit of worm on the end of a hook, nor anything like it—not they!

From *Storytelling on the Thames*, by Jerome K. Jerome (1888)

NO
TRESPASSING

Chapter Eleven

The Pursuit of Wounded Game:
To Trespass or Not

State v. Corbin, 343 N.W.2d 874 (Minn. 1984)

Ed Soost was operating the family farm in Minnesota when a hunting party, led by Jay Corbin and Ronald Niebuhr, approached him for permission to hunt his land. Soost told the hunters they could shoot in the woods, but that they could *not* go through the cornfield because of the damage to the crops they would cause.

The next day, the hunters returned and asked if they could get a wounded deer out of the cornfield. Soost absolutely *refused* permission for the hunters to retrieve the deer until he had the crop harvested.

Later that same day, Soost had a premonition about the deer hunters and went to his cornfield, where he discovered that they had in fact entered to retrieve the deer. Unfortunately, the cornfield was the only part of the Soost property that was *not* officially posted with "no trespassing" signs.

Soost called the sheriff's office, and Corbin and Niebuhr were charged with trespassing. At the pretrial conference, the judge indicated he would instruct the jury that a statute provided a defense to the trespassing charge—it clearly permitted a hunter to enter on *unposted* agricultural land in order to retrieve a wounded deer, even when told by the landowner *not* to do so. The state appealed the pretrial order.

This was a case of first impression, and the conundrum created by the conflict in hunting statutes was a curious one indeed. The prior statute provided that no person shall enter upon agricultural or nonagricultural land for hunting after being notified not to do so, either orally by the owner, occupant, or lessee, or by signs erected to that effect.

The next year the legislature passed a statute that provided that no person shall enter upon agricultural land for hunting unless the permission of the owner, occupant, or lessee was obtained. As part of the same legislative act, the statute was amended to create a limited exception for entry without permission to retrieve a wounded animal from agricultural lands that are *not* posted.

Corbin and Niebuhr obtained the initial permission necessary to enter upon Soost's land to hunt deer. Whether their subsequent entry into the cornfield to retrieve the wounded deer constituted a trespass depended upon the interpretation of the statute that allowed hunters to trespass in certain instances to retrieve a wounded animal *without permission* of the landowner.

The state interpreted "without permission" to mean "without having received a refusal." The defendants maintained that "without permission" allowed entry even after a refusal had been received.

In construing the statute, the court was aided by several principles. First, penal statutes must be construed strictly, and any reasonable doubt must be interpreted in favor of the defendant. Second, specific provisions of an act prevail over prior, general provisions. Finally, the court cannot provide that which the legislature purposely omitted or inadvertently overlooked.

In light of the misdemeanor penalty, this statute was clearly penal in nature. Second, the later statute was the more specific because it regulated a narrower range of activity. Finally, a plain reading of the entire statute suggested a purposeful omission of the construction urged by the state. The parallel subdivisions created gradations of protection and categories of notice, including written permission, oral permission, oral notice, and notice by posting signs.

The prior statute specifically provided two methods for a property owner to warn a hunter about trespassing—signs and oral notice. The later statute provided only one method of notice—posting. Therefore, the inference was clear that the legislature purposely omitted an oral notice provision.

The court remarked that this interpretation allowed limited entry on unposted *agricultural* land to retrieve a wounded animal after an oral notice *not* to do so, but would prohibit a similar entry on unposted *nonagricultural* land. Because the statute generally defined a more protected status for agricultural lands, a curious anomaly was created.

The court suggested that the legislature might address this issue in one of several ways: (a) require affirmative permission to enter agricultural land regardless of the presence of a wounded animal, (b) place greater weight on the refusal of permission to enter agricultural land, or (c) provide an additional limited exception for hunters to enter nonagricultural land to retrieve wounded animals. Until the legislature did so, the court concluded that statutory construction required the interpretation given by the trial court. In the meantime, if a landowner wished to avoid this temporary intrusion on agricultural land, he would have to post the land.

Mr. Soost therefore learned the hard way the value of erecting a cheap cardboard sign in front of his cornfield that simply stated: LIKE I SAID TO YOU BEFORE . . . NO TRESPASSING!

Hook & Bullet

Shooting a Walrus

No one who has not tried it will readily believe how extremely difficult it is to shoot an old bull-walrus clean dead. The front or sides of his head may be knocked all to pieces with bullets, and the animal yet have sense and strength sufficient left him to enable him to swim and dive out of reach. If he is lying on his side, with his back turned to his assailant, it is easy enough, as the brain is then quite exposed, and the crown of the head is easily penetrated; but one rarely gets the walrus in that position, and when it so happens, it is generally better policy to harpoon him without shooting.

By firing at an old bull directly facing you, it is almost impossible to kill him, but if half-front to you, a shot just above the eye may prove fatal. If sideways, he can only be killed by aiming about six inches behind the eye, and about one-fourth of the apparent depth of his head from the top; but the eye, of course, cannot be seen unless the animal is very close to you, and the difficulty is enormously increased by the back of the head being so embedded in fat, as to appear as if it were part of the neck.

If you hit him much below a certain part of the head you strike the jaw-joint, which is about the strongest part of the whole cranium. A leaden bullet striking there, or on the front of the head, is flattened like a piece of putty, without doing much injury to the walrus; and we sometimes found that even our hardened bullets, propelled by five drachms of powder, were broken into little pieces, against the rocky crania of these animals.

From *Sporting Adventures in the Northern Sea*, by James LaMont (1861)

Chapter Twelve

Fish Overboard: Recovering Lost Profits

Yarmouth Sea Products Ltd. v. Scully,
131 F.3d 389 (4th Cir. 1997)

At approximately 4:30 in the morning, with crystal clear skies and stars brightly visible overhead, the 65-foot sword-fishing boat *Lady Olive Marie* collided violently with the 60-foot racing sailboat *Coyote*. They were about 130 miles off the coast of Nova Scotia.

The wind at the time of the accident was "fresh," as they say in nautical circles—from the northeast at 25 to 35 knots—and the seas choppy—with waves of 10 to 15 feet. When the two craft crashed, *Lady Olive Marie* was drifting slowly at 1 to 1.5 knots with her engines in neutral, and *Coyote* was sailing downwind at a brisk 5 to 8 knots.

Lady Olive Marie was manned by a captain and six-member crew, and it was equipped with two properly operating radars (although, at the time of the collision, clutter obscured objects within a range of about two miles) and with fully functioning VHF and SSB marine radios. The boat also displayed properly illuminated navigation and fishing lights.

Coyote, on the other hand, was manned by a single sailor, David Scully, who, as part of a 2,000-mile qualifying voyage, was sailing from Horta, Azores, to Newport, Rhode Island, in order to compete in a race known as the "BOC Challenge Around the World Alone." *Coyote* was equipped with one radar, which was not operational due to failure of the electrical generator and to attempts by Scully to conserve battery power. Additionally, neither of the yacht's two VHF radios were in operation, and the mast-top navigation lights were not working.

When the vessels collided, the bowsprit of *Coyote* punctured the wooden hull of *Lady Olive Marie.* The wind blew the stern of *Coyote* around, bringing the vessels port to port and causing a rope from *Coyote* to become fouled in a part of *Lady Olive Marie*'s railing.

Shortly thereafter, *Lady Olive Marie*'s railing broke loose and the boats separated. After the vessels parted, Scully inexplicably failed to identify himself to the crew of *Lady Olive Marie* or ascertain whether they had sustained any damage. Not surprisingly, *Lady Olive Marie* quickly lost sight of *Coyote.*

Shortly after the casualty, the fish-hold of *Lady Olive Marie* began filling with water. The United States Coast Guard and the Canadian Coast Guard rendered assistance and eventually brought the capsize under control. Due to extensive damage, *Lady Olive Marie* was forced to return to port for repairs, resulting in abandonment of its fishing mission.

Under the terms of Yarmouth Company's agreement with the captain and crew members of *Lady Olive Marie*, Yarmouth would provide the vessel and the ice for the voyage in return for 40 percent of the catch, after being reimbursed for fuel, bait, and groceries. The crew, on the other hand, would fish the vessel for 60 percent of the catch, less the cost of fuel, bait, and groceries. Yarmouth would also pay the captain an additional 5 percent fee as compensation for his additional responsibilities.

After a two-day bench trial, the district court found Scully to be 100 percent at fault. The court awarded Yarmouth damages of

$78,616.81 for lost catch, loss of supplies, loss of brokerage, hull damage, and pre-judgment interest. Scully contended that the district court awarded damages which, as a matter of law, were not recoverable in a claim arising from a maritime collision, and that there was insufficient evidence of certain damages.

A venerable rule of admiralty jurisprudence is that a moving vessel is presumed to be at fault in a collision with a stationary, visible object. Scully argued that the district court improperly based its apportionment of fault on this presumption of negligence. The district court found that the *Coyote* was a moving vessel that collided with a stationary, visible object, and consequently required him to show by clear and convincing evidence that his conduct could not have contributed to the accident.

Scully argued vigorously that this was error. He maintained that because *Lady Olive Marie* was adrift and not stationary, the presumption was inapplicable.

The appellate court agreed with Scully that *Lady Olive Marie* was not stationary within the meaning of the relevant statutory provision, and that the presumption of fault was not appropriate. The record revealed that *Lady Olive Marie* met the statutory definition of a power driven vessel "underway" in that it was not "at anchor, or made fast to the shore, or aground." Thus, the arguably relevant statutory standard provided that a power-driven vessel underway should keep out of the way of a sailing vessel.

Scully also contended that the district court erred in its determinations as to the proper elements and amounts of damages. With one exception (dealing with lost profits), the appellate court rejected those challenges. Scully was especially adamant that Yarmouth's claim for lost catch was simply speculative to support an award of damages as a matter of law.

The appellate court held that the loss of profits or the use of a vessel pending repairs, or other detention, arising from a colli-

sion or other maritime tort was a proper element of damage, and the issue was too well settled to be open to question. The court noted, however, that it was equally well settled that such damages will only be allowed when profits have actually been, or are reasonably supposed to have been, lost, and the amount of such profits is proven with reasonable certainty.

The key to recovery in such cases is the ability to prove loss of profits "with reasonable certainty." What constitutes reasonable certainty is, of necessity, a fact-intensive inquiry to be determined on a case-by-case basis. Scully maintained that even if the claim for lost catch is one on which relief can be granted, the damages had not, as a matter of law, been proven with reasonable certainty.

Scully further maintained that while such damages were normally measured by taking a fair average of a vessel's earnings over a number of voyages before and after the collision, in this case the district court's ultimate award bore an insufficient relationship to the four voyages offered in evidence by Yarmouth.

Notwithstanding this evidence, the district court concluded that the actual catch and actual revenues of a boat called *Endurance* were the best evidence of how much *Lady Olive Marie* would have caught on this voyage. *Endurance* fished the same area at the same time that *Lady Olive Marie* would have. Yet the record contained undisputed evidence that although *Lady Olive Marie* often fished alongside *Endurance*, the two boats' catches varied greatly.

Moreover, in making its award, the district court did not give any consideration to the previous four voyages of *Lady Olive Marie* offered in evidence. Rather, the court simply awarded Yarmouth damages in the amount of fish sold by *Endurance*. This figure, however, represented some $25,000 more than the average earnings of *Lady Olive Marie*, and $10,000 more than that vessel's best catch of the year.

Lady Olive Marie had caught no fish at the time of the collision. Therefore, the appellate court held that the district court's reliance on the catch of *Endurance*, without so much as a reference to the evidence of the four other *Lady Olive Marie*'s voyages, suggested a lack of reasonable certainty in the damage award.

Without a reasoned explanation for using the voyage of *Endurance* as an appropriate measure of damage for lost catch, the appellate court was unable to conclude that the award of damages was supported by reasonable certainty. Accordingly, the court vacated the judgment and remanded this portion of the damage award for further consideration.

As a result, the amount of damages for hull repair to *Lady Olive Marie* remained easily quantifiable. But the question of how many fish she would have caught if she had remained afloat became a much more, shall we say, esoteric proposition.

Hook & Bullet

Psychic Rewards

And for the lawfulness of fishing, it may very well be maintained by our Savior's bidding St. Peter cast his hook into the water and caught a fish for money to pay tribute to Caesar. And let me tell you that angling is of high esteem and of much use in other nations. He that reads the voyages of Ferdinand Mendez Pinto shall find that there he declares to have found a king and several priests a-fishing.

And he that reads Plutarch shall find that angling was not contemptible in the days of Marc Antony and Cleopatra and that they in the midst of their wonderful glory used angling as a principal recreation. And let me tell you that in the Scripture angling is always taken in the best sense and that though hunting may be sometimes so taken, yet it is but seldom to be so understood. And let me add this more. He that views the ancient ecclesiastical canons shall find hunting to be forbidden to churchmen, as being a toilsome, perplexing recreation; and shall find angling allowed to clergymen, as being a harmless recreation, a recreation that invites them to contemplation and quietness.

From *The Compleat Angler*, by Izaak Walton (1653)

Chapter Thirteen

Animal Sacrifice: Free Exercise Ramifications

Church of Lukumi Babalu Aye v. City of Hialeah, 508 U.S. 520 (1993)

The right to kill animals can create some interesting line drawing.

Hunting is permitted in every state in the country (with certain restrictions, of course), and some of these shooting sports are pursued mostly for food, and others strictly for sport. In spite of the ability to kill animals, there are numerous state and federal statutes preventing cruelty to them. And then there is the issue of animal sacrifice for religious purposes.

A church in South Florida known as the Lukumi Babalu Aye practices the Santeria religion, and it has an estimated 50,000 practitioners. The Santeria religion originated in the nineteenth century and employs animal sacrifice as one of its principal forms of devotion.

Sacrifices are performed at births, marriages, and funerals; for the cure of the sick; for the initiation of new members and priests; and during an annual celebration. Animals sacrificed in Santeria rituals include chickens, pigeons, doves, ducks, guinea pigs, goats, sheep, and turtles. The animals are killed by the cutting of the carotid arteries, and the sacrificed animal is usually cooked and eaten.

The church announced plans to establish a house of worship as well as a school, cultural center, and museum in Hialeah, Florida, and the pastor proclaimed that the church's goal was to bring its ritual of animal sacrifice into the open. The church then began to obtain the necessary licenses, inspections, and zoning approvals. Many members of the Hialeah community found the prospect of an animal-sacrificing church distressing, and so the city council held an emergency public session.

First of all, the city council adopted Resolution 87-66, which noted the "concern" expressed by residents "that certain religions may propose to engage in practices which are inconsistent with public morals, peace or safety," and that the city "reiterates its commitment to a prohibition against any and all acts of any and all religious groups which are inconsistent with public morals, peace or safety."

The council then pronounced Resolution 87-90, which reaffirmed its residents' "great concern regarding the possibility of public ritualistic animal sacrifices" and noted the prohibition by state law. The resolution declared the city policy "to oppose the ritual sacrifices of animals," and announced that any person or organization practicing animal sacrifice "will be prosecuted."

A number of ordinances were then passed by the city council:

- Ordinance 87-40 incorporated the Florida animal cruelty laws and noted that they had been interpreted to include killings for religious reasons;
- Ordinance 87-52 defined "sacrifice" as "unnecessarily killing animal in a ritual not for the primary purpose of food consumption," and prohibited the "possession, sacrifice, or slaughter" of an animal if killed in "any type of ritual";
- Ordinance 87-71 prohibited the sacrifice of animals; and

- Ordinance 87-72 prohibited slaughter of animals outside of areas zoned for slaughterhouses.

Following the enactment of these ordinances, the church filed suit against the city in federal district court. Alleging violations of its rights under the free exercise clause, the complaint sought declaratory judgment and injunctive and monetary relief. The federal district court ruled for the city, finding no violation of the church's rights under the free exercise clause.

Acknowledging that "the ordinances are not religiously neutral," and that the city's concern about animal sacrifice was "prompted" by the establishment of the church in the city, the district court concluded that the purpose of the ordinances was not to exclude the church from the city, but to end the practice of animal sacrifice. The court concluded that, at most, the ordinances' effect on the petitioners' religious conduct was "incidental to their secular purpose and effect."

The district court proceeded to determine whether the governmental interests underlying the ordinances were compelling. It found four: First, the court found a substantial health risk because animals to be sacrificed were often kept in unsanitary conditions. Second, the court found emotional injury to children who witnessed these sacrifices. Third, the court found compelling the city's interest in protecting animals from cruel and unnecessary killing. Fourth, the court found compelling the city's interest in restricting the slaughter of animals to areas so zoned.

The Court of Appeals for the Eleventh Circuit affirmed the lower court's decision in a one-paragraph *per curiam* opinion. The appellate court stated simply that it concluded the ordinances were consistent with the Constitution.

In its brief, the city conceded that neither the State of Florida nor the city had enacted a generally applicable ban on the killing of animals. It asserted, however, that animal sacrifice was "different" from animal killings permitted by law. According to the city, it was "self-evident" that killing animals for food was "important," and that the euthanasia of excess animals "made sense."

Justice Kennedy delivered the opinion of the United States Supreme Court, which concluded that the laws in question were enacted contrary to free-exercise principles and were therefore void. Under the free-exercise clause, a law that burdens religious practice need not be justified by a compelling governmental interest if it is neutral and of general applicability. Otherwise, it must undergo the most rigorous of scrutiny—it must be justified by a compelling governmental interest, and it must be narrowly tailored to advance that interest.

The Court noted that the ordinances' texts and operation demonstrated they were not neutral, but had as their object the suppression of the church's central element, which was animal sacrifice. The fact that religious exercise had been targeted was evidenced by Resolution 87-66's statements of "concern" and "commitment," and by the use of the words "sacrifice" and "ritual" in Ordinances 87-40, 87-52, and 87-71. The ordinances' various prohibitions, definitions, and exemptions demonstrated that they were "gerrymandered" to proscribe religious killings of animals by church members, and excluded almost all other animal killings.

The Court also held that the ordinances suppressed much more religious conduct than was necessary to achieve their stated ends. The legitimate governmental interests in protecting the public health and preventing cruelty to animals could be addressed by restrictions far short of a flat prohibition of all sacrificial practices. Examples cited were general regulations for the disposal of organic garbage, for the care of animals regardless of why they were kept, and for methods of slaughter.

The ordinances therefore could not withstand strict scrutiny.

They were not narrowly tailored to accomplish the asserted governmental interests. All four were overbroad or underinclusive in substantial respects because the objectives were not pursued with respect to analogous nonreligious conduct, and those interests could be achieved by narrower ordinances.

Accordingly, the neutrality inquiry led to but one conclusion: the ordinances had as their object the suppression of religion. The pattern disclosed animosity to church adherents and their religious practices; the ordinances, by their own terms, targeted this religious exercise; the texts of the ordinances were gerrymandered with care to proscribe religious killings of animals, but to exclude almost all secular killings; and the ordinances suppressed much more religious conduct than necessary to achieve the legitimate ends asserted. These ordinances, the Court noted, were clearly *not* neutral.

The Court concluded that each of the ordinances pursued the city's governmental interests only against conduct motivated by religious belief. The ordinances had "every appearance of a prohibition that society is prepared to impose upon [Santeria worshippers], but not upon itself."

To satisfy the commands of the First Amendment, a law restrictive of religious practice must advance "interests of the highest order" and must be narrowly tailored in pursuit of those interests. A law that targets religious conduct for distinctive treatment or advances legitimate governmental interests only against conduct with a religious motivation will survive strict scrutiny only in rare cases.

The city ordinances in question were therefore rendered void. As a result, animal-sacrifice hunters were granted the same rights as those of their less religious brethren.

About the Author

Cecil C. Kuhne III is a litigator in the Dallas office of Fulbright & Jaworski L.L.P. He has spent considerable time behind various guns and fishing rods, but when searching for a term to describe his skills in these pursuits, the word *proficient* does not readily spring to mind.

Index